CW00547497

J. & A. Gardner & Co Ltd
Shipowners and Quarrymasters

by

Graham Atkinson

INTRODUCTION

I grew up in Blyth, a port which once held the British record for coal shipped in one year. Consequently, my interest in shipping centred on colliers and coastal ships. It was through my work that I became acquainted with their crews. As the number of these ships declined through sales and scrapping, I began to research the history of individual vessels and then companies. My interest in J. & A. Gardner & Co Ltd arose from a curiosity to find out what happened to their ships that had been regular callers in Blyth. David Burrell very kindly gave me the fleet list he had researched some years earlier, and I am very grateful for his help and advice in starting my research.

The history of J. & A. Gardner & Co Ltd is linked to the rise of industrial Glasgow during the late 19th century and the decline of small Irish Sea ports in the 20th century. James Gardner took out a lease on the granite quarry at Bonawe during the 1870s and this proved to be the cornerstone on which the company's fortunes were founded. With the growth of Clydeside came the demand for building materials needed for housing, factories and roads - all of which required granite in their construction. Throughout the first half of the 20th century, the Gardner fleet loaded coal for Ireland in west coast ports of the United Kingdom and if another cargo was not readily available, the ship would be sent to Bonawe to load granite for Glasgow. The company was one of the first British shipowners to order a motor ship yet it remained faithful to the steam coaster until 1959.

The advent of containerisation and the centralisation of port facilities during the latter half of the 20th century saw the demise of small quays and ports in the Irish Sea area, and the company looked to replace cargoes lost. Consequently they entered the Baltic timber trade and then began to specialise in heavy-lift and indivisible cargoes. With the increase in indivisible loads shipped around the coast of the United Kingdom, Gardners ordered four vessels between 1973 and 1980 capable of loading both bulk and roll-on/roll-off cargoes and thus created a niche service to customers until the late 1990s.

The company has remained a family one throughout its history. James Gardner's son, John, had no family and he took his nephews, James and Alexander Struthers, into the business. It is Alexander's son and granddaughter who now manage the company in 2002 on a much-reduced scale. I would like here to record my thanks to both of them for their help in writing this history of their company and family. The late Malcolm Glen, who worked for the company for many years until his sudden death in 2001, answered many of my questions and was a mine of information which I was able to tap into. I am only sorry that he did not see this book published. I hope that he would have been happy with the finished work.

Graham Atkinson, Blyth, August 2002

PUBLISHER'S NOTE

Every effort has been made to ensure the photographs are correctly credited. We apologise in advance if correct credit has not been given. Some photographs in the collections of the author and the publisher do not bear the name of the photographer and these have been credited to the respective collections. In both the narrative and the fleet list, in order to assist readers in identifying which vessel is being referred to, the suffix (1), (2) etc has been occasionally added after a ship's name to indicate that this is the first, second etc vessel to bear this name.

Copyright © 2002 by Graham Atkinson and Bernard McCall. The right of Graham Atkinson and Bernard McCall to be identified as authors of this work has been asserted by them in accordance with the Copyright, Design and Patent Act 1998.

All rights reserved. No part of this publication may be reproduced, stored in a retrieval system or transmitted in any form or by any means (electronic, digital, mechanical, photocopying, recording or otherwise) without prior permission of the publisher.

Published by Bernard McCall, 400 Nore Road, Portishead, Bristol, BS20 8EZ, England.
Telephone/fax : 01275 846178. e-mail : bmccall@globalnet.co.uk
All distribution enquiries should be addressed to the publisher.

Printed by Sebright Printers, 12 - 18 Stokes Croft, Bristol, BS1 3PR

ISBN : 1-902953-07-X

Front cover : Ships of the Gardner fleet were regular callers at various ports on the Manchester Ship Canal. The two photographs on the front cover were taken at the western end of the Canal during the late summer of 1977 and illustrate the fact that the company did not have a standard hull livery for its ships. In the upper photograph, the grey-hulled **Saint William** *approaches Eastham Locks while the lower photograph depicts a black-hulled (and work stained!)* **Saint Aidan** *at a similar location.*
(Both photographs by Neil Burns)

..., Gardner quarry. **Saint Oran** *was photographed on 7 April 1986 as she loaded tarred roadstone at ...tive.*
(Bernard McCall)

A FAMILY BUSINESS

James Gardner was born in 1829 at Larbert; his parents were James Gardner, a builder, and Janet Davie Gardner. By the time he was twenty one, young James had moved to Glasgow and had become a master flesher living at 20, Hill Place, Stirling Road, Glasgow. In December 1850 he married Helen MacGregor Young from Tillicoultry, Fife, who was three years his senior. Her parents were James and Barbara Young, nee MacGregor, who claimed to be descended from the famous Rob Roy MacGregor, who was immortalised in the book by Sir Walter Scott, through his illegitimate son. James' and Helen's marriage resulted in nine children : George (born about 1851), James (born about 1852), John (born 1853), Alexander (born 1855), Janet Davie (born 1857), Duncan MacGregor (born1857), Peter (born 1860), Helen Young (born 1861) and Barbara (born 1862).

In 1873 James and his family moved to Ballachulish after he had taken a fifteen-year lease on the slate quarries there, trading as Ballachulish Slate Quarries. His son George was now a solicitor and acted for the quarry's proprietor Lady Beresford of Ballachulish. Ballachulish on the southern shores of Loch Leven was a remote settlement, the nearest major town being Fort William on the north eastern shore of Loch Linnhe, at the foot of Ben Nevis. Ballachulish Slate Quarries were agents for the Bank of Scotland & North British Mercantile Insurance Co and James and his family lived at Laroch House, Ballachulish.

This photograph of James Gardner is sadly undated.   *(Company archives)*

In 1876 James ordered a small steamship to enable him to carry quarried slate from Ballachulish to industrial Glasgow, returning with cargoes required for the remote Argyll settlements. James opened an office at 43, Renfield Street, Glasgow, as a shipping agent and in 1879 J. & A. Gardner was formed as a partnership by his sons John and Alexander with offices at 21 Clyde Place. John moved to Glasgow taking up residence at 3 Afton Close, while Alexander remained in Argyll to oversee the quarries. The new company also operated the Lettermore granite quarry at Ballachulish and in 1882 they began working the Kintallen and Lagnaha quarries. In 1885 J. & A. Gardner & Co was formed. The company remained at 21 Clyde Place although John had moved residence to 114 Montrose Street. In the following year, 1886, James moved his shipping agency to 21 Clyde Place. The company's entry for the Glasgow Postal Address Book describes them as 'granite and quartz quarrymasters and monumental masons with quarries at Lettermore, Kintallen and Lagnaha, Ballachulish'.

Although the lease on the Ballachulish quarry was for fifteen years George Gardner altered the lease to twenty five years. This resulted in a court case between Lady Beresford and the Gardners which found in favour of Lady Beresford. The Gardners left Ballachulish in 1892 and moved south to work the Ardchattan, Bonawe and Craigpoint quarries at Bonawe on the shores of Loch Etive.

At the entrance to Loch Etive, under Connel Bridge, the channel is one cable wide and there is a ledge across the sound that dries in the centre at low tide. At low water springs the water level outside is four feet lower than the ledge and the outgoing water runs in channels on both sides of the dry ledge and is referred to as Connel Falls or the Falls of Lora where, during spring tides, the rate of the stream is up to six knots. Further up Loch Etive at Bonawe Narrows the stream is up to two and a half knots. In the first half of the eighteenth century charcoal making and iron smelting began in the Highlands.

Around 1753 a Lancaster company erected a furnace at Taynuilt for casting pig ore, taking leases on several farms to graze their workhorses and for the forests of trees which they used to create charcoal. Iron ore was shipped to the site from Lancashire, while the company used either birch or oak from their farms to make into charcoal. Under the title of the Iron Furnace Company smelting continued at Bonawe, near Taynuilt, until the mid-1800s. The company also diversified, making gunpowder for a short time at Melford although the practice ended in 1867 following an explosion.

The granite quarried at Bonawe on Loch Etive was sold as chippings for roadmaking and granite setts for tramways. It also made excellent building stone. The waste material from the setts was sold as granolithic for making pavements. Some of this was used in Oban and even after 100 years it is still in good condition. Granite setts from Bonawe were used in the construction of the Glasgow tramways and for the construction of new roads. Granite setts were also used in Glasgow's King George V Bridge and the construction of both entrances to the Mersey tunnel. Further up the Loch, at the Craig quarries, the granite was a coarser type and was extracted in blocks and used for building and harbour works.

There was little mechanisation at that time. Steam cranes were not used until the turn of the century, so granite was wheeled to the ship in barrows and tipped into the hold. At the peak of productivity the quarries employed several hundred men although this number dropped as tarmacadam was used in road construction.

In 1892 James' son, Duncan MacGregor Gardner, entered shipowning in his own right when he purchased the steamer **Cuirassier**, sharing the same address as his brothers at 21 Clyde Place. Unfortunately this small vessel was lost in 1894 and Duncan replaced her with another steamship, **Helen MacGregor**, purchased from his father. **Helen MacGregor** was lost in 1897 and Duncan later emigrated to South America. His brother George also emigrated, to Canada, and died in April 1937. James' daughters Helen Young Gardner, Janet Davie Gardner and Barbara Gardner remained in Scotland all their lives. Helen remained a spinster and died in December 1945 at Baldernock.

Janet, known as Jessie to her family, became the second wife of Alexander Fulton Struthers who was a pavement merchant. By coincidence Alexander Fulton's first wife Janet Dunlop Struthers, nee Steel, was also known as Jessie. She bore Alexander two children, Thomas Struthers (born 1879) and Janet Fulton Struthers (born 1881). Unfortunately both Jessie and her daughter died before 1883 and Alexander was left to bring up his infant son. Janet and Alexander married on 25 March 1884 in Lagnaha, Duror, Argyll, and had three children. Again, tragically, the middle child, Helen, died in infancy leaving the couple with two sons, James Gardner Struthers (born 1885), who was born at Strathaven, Lanarkshire, and Alexander Fulton Struthers (born 1887), born in Govan. Alexander Struthers died in 1888 and Janet Davie Struthers and her sons were looked after by her family in Scotland and Canada. For six months of the year she and her sons lived in Canada with George. They spent the other half of the year with her parents and brothers in Scotland.

Both John and Alexander had also married, John to Isabel Allison and Alexander to Janet Gibson Graham. Both marriages produced no children. Helen MacGregor Gardner died on 5 March 1895 at Lagnaha and James Gardner died in 1903. Alexander Gardner died on 5 May 1897 after he fell asleep in his bed while smoking a cigar that consequently started a fire. In 1896 J. & A. Gardner & Co moved its offices to 19 Commerce Street and in 1903 moved again to 65 Great Clyde Street. John Gardner had also moved residence twice - in 1895 to 19 Clifford Street, Paisley Road, and in 1900 to the United Free Manse in Kilbarchan.

As John Gardner had no heirs, he took his nephews James Gardner Struthers and Alexander Fulton Struthers into the company which became a limited company on 28 April 1906. Mr McConnachie, the Secretary of the new company, was instructed to agree a price and terms for the transfer of the company to limited status. After converting to a limited company, John Gardner became the sole Director and Manager. On 11 July 1906, the first seven shares in the limited company were issued singularly as below:

John Gardner	(Quarrymaster & Shipowner), Forehouse, Kilbarchan	
William Gillies	(Writer) 204 West George Street, Glasgow	
Alexander Duff Menzies	(Writer) " "	
John McConnachie	(Writer) " "	
William McDonald Alexander	(Writer) " "	
James Gardner Struthers	(Chemist) 244 West Princes Street, Glasgow	
Alexander Fulton Struthers	(Clerk) " "	

John Gardner.

(Company archives)

The four writers, or solicitors, belonged to the firm of John Steuart & Gillies, Glasgow. John Gardner received a further 45,000 shares in the limited company on 27 September 1906 in respect of the sale and transfer of the business of J. & A. Gardner & Co to the limited company. The limited company was allowed to operate at Bonawe from Whit Sunday, 1906 following the creation of a new twenty five-year lease. John Gardner had a £5,000 share in the old lease which was exchanged for a further 5,000 shares in the limited company, initially receiving two further lots of 500 shares. The two ships included in the sale, **Wharfinger** and **Bonawe** (1), were valued at £1500 over £2000, being the balance of a £5000 mortgage on **Wharfinger**. **Bonawe** was valued at a straight £5,000. The new company retained its predecessor's office at 65 Great Clyde Street. Following the renaming and renumbering of the street in 1930 by Glasgow Corporation it became 228 Clyde Street where the company remained until 25 June 1993. On 13 January 1908 a resolution was passed that no shares be offered for public subscription and that the number of members, i.e. shareholders, be limited to fifty, not excluding company employees. Control of the company's share capital effectively remained within the Gardner and Struthers families.

In February 1912 the company applied to Clydesdale Bank for an overdraft facility of £6,000 to allow it to build workers' homes at Bonawe using the steamers **Saint Modan** (1), **Bonawe**, **Ardchattan** and **Ardachy** as surety against the loan. The accounts for the company's financial year to 31 October 1911 reported its first profits when it made a surplus of £162 8s 11d (£162.44). This increased to £861 13s 4½d (£861.67) in 1912 due to a sharp rise in freight rates. Profits increased steadily and small dividends, usually of around 3%, were paid to shareholders with the remaining profits put into reserve to cover poor trading years in the future. Profits rose dramatically during World War 1, the company's accounts showing a profit of £17,000 16s 6½d (£17,000.83) to the year end 31 October 1916 with a dividend of £6,900 paid to shareholders. During World War 2, the company found itself in a similar position with the February 1941 AGM reporting a profit of £98,808 16s 9d (£98,808.84) after an income tax bill of £66,631 18s 7d (£66,631.93) had been paid. A dividend of £13,227 was declared on paid up stock and £85,531 16s 6d (£85,531.83) was carried forward, presumably to pay for replacement tonnage required during 1940.

During World War 1 James Struthers served as a pilot in the Royal Naval Air Service rising to the rank of Major. He became a skilled airship pilot and sank several German U-boats for which he received the Distinguished Service Cross and two Bars. He was also credited as having flown the greatest number of hours in airships during the war. Alexander served in France as a Captain in the Cameronian Scottish Rifles and was wounded three times. He was awarded the Military Cross.

Following the end of World War 1, there was a great boom in shipping. War losses had been high due to the German U-boat offensive and there was an acute shortage of available tonnage. High freight rates increased shipowner's profits and shipbuilders were able to charge inflated prices for new tonnage. The eventual downturn saw many owners go out of business because their ships, ordered on the back of high freight rates, could not earn enough to repay their building costs. In 1921, the company's accounts showed a profit of £59,778 5s 8½d (£59,778.28), compared to only £860 nine years previously, with £11,500 being paid in dividends to shareholders. The accounts warned that the company might be liable to pay tax on excess profits and no dividend was paid the following year, £23,600 being put aside should a claim be forthcoming. Profits continued to reflect the economic difficulties of the period, £5,099 14s 4d (£5,099.72) in 1926, and the policy of placing profits in reserve to see the company through poor trading years ensured the company's survival while others failed.

John Gardner was appointed Chairman for life on Friday 27 November 1931 with a salary of £1,000 per annum, payable in two instalments on 30 April and 31 October of each year which was backdated to 30 April 1931. On the same day James Gardner Struthers and Alexander Fulton Struthers became Directors, both now holding 23,001 company shares as a result of John Gardner transferring some of his shareholding to them. John Gardner died on 15 February 1932 at Woodend House, Bridge of Weir. Control of J. & A. Gardner & Co Ltd passed to his two nephews, and although neither assumed the title of Chairman, as the eldest James Struthers chaired meetings and AGMs. Alexander Struthers became company secretary in January 1935 following the death of Mr McConnachie, whose nominal single share passed to Mr E. Dunlop, a partner in John Steuart & Gillies.

In November 1935, a resolution allowing the appointment of Trustees for the holders of company shares was passed, subject to a Deed Trust being approved by the Directors and Trustees. As a result £46,007 was converted to £1 shares and was issued to shareholders according to their shareholding at 31 October 1935 and all the issue was placed in the Trust Fund, administered by Mr W. J. Taylor, a solicitor, and Mr A. E. Smith, a chartered accountant. The Trustees also received a nominal single company share. Mr Taylor died in February 1936 and was replaced as a Trustee by Mr J. Patterson.

James Struthers resigned as a director of the company on 26 October 1937. He had married Enid Huntington who was some twenty five years his junior in 1936. After their marriage they embarked on a round the world cruise. They had three children, Helen MacGregor Struthers (born 1938), Enid Janet Struthers (born 1940) and Charles Huntington Struthers (born 1944). Mr Struthers and his wife settled in Ardmaddy which is to the north of Bonawe on the shores of Loch Etive, where their two youngest children were born, Helen MacGregor Struthers having been born in Sydney, Australia. James Struthers took no further part in the company's business, although he retained a single nominal company share and he died, aged 94, on 29 April 1978 at Ardmaddy. His widow, who is alive to date, and three children survived him.

Alexander Struthers was left as the sole Director in charge of the day to day running of the company and Minute Books show only he and the auditor's representative present at subsequent AGMs. In order to buy his brother's share of the business Alexander borrowed money from the Clydesdale Bank who took James Struthers' remaining 23,000 shares as security. These were transferred to Alexander Struthers' ownership in 1941 after the loan had been repaid.

Alexander Fulton Struthers had married Elizabeth Margaret Hutchison on 11 June 1919. Her father, William Hutchison, had at one time been Conservative MP for the Glasgow district of Kelvingrove and they had three sons, John Gardner Struthers (born 1922), William Hutchinson Struthers (born 1925), and Alastair 'Sandy' James Struthers (born 1929). John and William were killed in World War 2; John was a Sub Lieutenant on **HMS Kite** which was part of the escort for Convoy JW59, sailing from the Clyde for the Kola Inlet. In the early hours of 21 August 1944 **HMS Kite** was struck by two torpedoes from U344 and sank in one minute and there were only nine survivors. William was killed on 26 April 1945, days before the war in Europe ended while serving with the Scots Guards in Germany.

Alastair Struthers was only sixteen when the War ended and his father was not sure if he would enter the business. So, unlike other owners, the company did not order or buy any replacements for their war losses. In March 1945 Alexander Struthers transferred 2,000 shares to his wife, who was also appointed a Director with an annual salary of £150. Mr Alexander Struthers was also confirmed as the Company Secretary, having 'been acting in that capacity for some time past'. His combined salary for both posts was set at £1,400 per annum. During 1947 Mr & Mrs Struthers spent some time in America on a business trip and in their absence Mr James Shaw Wilson, who had become a Trustee in place of Mr A. E. Smith in February 1945, was appointed a Director of the company.

When he was eighteen, Alastair Struthers joined the army for two years National Service having been educated at Stowe and served in the Cameronian Scottish Rifles as a 2nd Lieutenant. On completion of his army service he went to Trinity College, Cambridge, in October 1949 where he studied for an M. A. degree until 1952. He returned to Glasgow to become involved in the running of the company and became a Director on 29 July 1953. Mr Alexander Struthers continued to reduce his shareholding in favour of his wife and son. In 1953 the shareholding in the company stood at:

Mr A. F. Struthers   17,336 shares
Mr A. J. Struthers   21,335 shares
Mrs E. M. Struthers   9,335 shares

Alastair Struthers succeeded his father as Company Secretary on 18 April 1957. Mr Wilson died in 1960 and Alexander Struthers, Alastair Struthers and Mrs Struthers continued as Board members, with Alexander and Alastair Struthers conducting the day-to-day business. Alexander Struthers died on 25 April 1963 and was succeeded as Chairman by his son who by resolution also acquired his father's 17,336 company shares.

In 1965 Gardners acquired a 50% shareholding in the Ardrossan based shipping agency R. L. Alpine & Co, with the remaining shares acquired by Glenlight Shipping Ltd. Alpines had been formed in 1877 by Robert Alpine who was succeeded by his son, George, who remained in the business until his retirement in 1964. An office was opened at Irvine in 1921 to handle the increase in trade there. Alpines became a private limited company with assets of £10,000 on 7 May 1949.

On 18 August 1965 William Stevens succeeded Alastair Struthers as Company Secretary, Alastair continuing as Chairman. In 1967 Alastair Struthers married Miss Elizabeth Pitcairn Henderson, daughter of Morrice and Mary Henderson, in London on 17 October. They have three daughters, Stephanie Mary (born 1968), Annabel Jane (born 1970) and Elizabeth Lorna (born 1973). Mrs Struthers' middle name has its origins from the Scottish town of the same name. One of her forebears was the lookout whose ship first sighted the Pitcairn Islands. The name of his home town was given to the newly-discovered islands which later found fame after the **Bounty** mutineers settled there. In 1974 Mrs. Struthers entered the business becoming a Director and Company Secretary in succession to Mr. Stevens.

1969 was the first year in which the shipping turnover exceeded that of the quarries and in 1973 shipping turnover exceeded £1 million for the first time. The 1970s proved to be a difficult time for the company. In 1975 an unusually high number of surveys were carried out on the fleet which affected profitability, and 1976 saw a depressed freight market. The profitability of two vessels, **Saint Ronan** (2) and **Saint Fergus**, was dependent on the performance of the quarries, which was poor, and the rest of the fleet had to trade well to offset the pair's trading results. During 1977 the quarries' performance improved, sales increasing from £203,000 to £344,000 for the year ending October 1977 with tonnage up from 38,000 to 55,000 tons.

On 1 April 1976 William Leitch was appointed to the Board as a Director. Mr Leitch had joined the company as a seagoing engineer before coming ashore to become Gardner's Engineering Superintendent. His twin brother Hugh had served as master in Gardners' ships and he too came ashore as the company's Marine Superintendent. Throughout the 1970s the company faced many problems which affected its profitability. Low freight rates, increased crew wages and the Middle Eastern oil crisis all took their toll. In 1978 the company recorded a trading loss citing the fact that several ships had undergone major drydocking during the year and three ships had also been caught by a strike in the Manchester Ship Canal.

Leased new equipment at Bonawe helped production, but while quarry sales figures were similar to the previous year costs had increased. The quarries relied heavily on the Shetland Islands Council and Western Isles for the bulk of their orders and the major concern was the cost of bitumen, used in the making of tarred chippings, which included oil in its content. The rising price of oil affected the cost of coated stone in addition to all company activities and the freight market remained at a level where it could not carry large cost increases.

Major Gardner's son, Charles Huntingdon Struthers, who had been running the quarry operations at Bonawe for some time, joined the Board as a Director on 1 August 1981 which now comprised Alastair Struthers, his wife Mrs Elizabeth P. Struthers, his mother Mrs Elizabeth M. Struthers, Charles H. Struthers and William Leitch. On 22 April 1983 Mrs E. P. Struthers resigned as Company Secretary and was succeeded by chartered accountant Mr Ronald McKenzie Bell.

J. & A. Gardner & Co (Management) Ltd was incorporated with a capital of £100 on 13 December 1979 for the purpose of supplying personnel for J. & A. Gardner & Co Ltd's vessels and third party companies. For a short time in 1984 J. & A. Gardner & Co (Management) Ltd was the nominal owner of the four ships operated by Gardners. In an attempt to reduce operating costs, Gardner Shipping (Scotland) Ltd was incorporated on 25 September 1981 to charter the J. & A. Gardner & Co Ltd fleet. Because J. & A. Gardner & Co Ltd was a member of the General Council of British Shipping they had to pay any wage rises which had been agreed with the unions. The company's vessels were therefore classed as being federated. Because Gardner Shipping (Scotland) Ltd was not part of the GCBS, any ships owned or chartered by them could operate outside the confines of the GCBS. Gardners had a choice at this time. They could remain a member of the GCBS and possibly cease trading because of competition and rising costs or they could de-federate and survive as a lone player.

On 16 September 1983 the share capital of J. & A. Gardner & Co Ltd was increased from 50,000 to 92,014 shares, by the creation of 42,014 shares of £1 each. At this time there were only three shareholders, Alastair Struthers who held 35,672, his wife and his mother, each holding 500 and 9,835 shares respectively. Mrs Elizabeth M. Struthers died on 2 February 1989 and later that year Alastair Struthers' eldest daughter Stephanie became a Director as of 1 June.

The poor economic conditions continued into the early 1980s and the sale of the older general cargo ships, replaced by a fleet of three multi purpose vessels, helped the company retain a positive cash flow. In 1982 a net profit before taxation of £514,713 was recorded which included the sale of two ships although a rise of 25% rise in freight rates was required to cover capital and interest rises. Gardners had borrowed money to pay for four new ships and were liable for leasing payments to the mortgage companies which were a considerable strain on finances. Freight rates remained depressed for the next two years. The 1984 AGM reported a loss of £102,294 which was deducted from the adjusted balance of Retained Profits. The company's financial reserves were slowly being eroded because the fleet was not earning enough to pay capital repayments on loans, a situation perfectly normal within the industry.

Following the end of the Falklands conflict in 1982, **Saint Brandan** (4) was chartered by the Ministry of Defence for service around the Falkland Islands. **Saint Angus** (3) replaced her at the end of her original charter and **Saint Brandan** returned to the South Atlantic in 1988 and has continued on this charter to the present day.

Saint Brandan *arrives at Marchwood military jetty, Southampton Water. The occasion was her return from service in the Falkland Islands.*
(Company archives)

Changes in Corporation Tax in 1985 could have benefitted the company by £250,000 during the next five years but wages and fuel costs continued to be the main problems facing the company. Fortunately low fuel costs contributed to better results reported in October 1986. The Oban based plant hire firm of C. J. MacKinnon Ltd was purchased for £25,000 on 27 October 1989 and a further £9,000 was required to clear creditors and liabilities. The purchase was seen as one to complement the existing quarrying and construction activities but did not prove so and on 31 October 1990 C. J. MacKinnon Ltd and J. & A. Gardner & Co (Management) Ltd were both closed down. Both companies' assets were transferred to J. & A. Gardner & Co Ltd and the group was able to make tax savings with less active companies.

Mr Malcolm Glen and Mr Alastair Tear were appointed as Directors of Gardner Shipping (Scotland) Ltd. in November 1990. Both were long serving managers with Gardners. Mr Glen joined the company in 1961 from Clan Line Steamers Ltd and Mr Tear in 1975, becoming Managing Director of J. & A. Gardner & Co Ltd on 11 March 1993. Following his retirement William Leitch resigned as a Director of both J. & A. Gardner & Co Ltd and J. & A. Gardner (Scotland) Ltd on 1 October 1993. Both he and his brother Hugh remain connected with the company as consultants in their respective fields.

The April 1992 AGM reported a group Retained Profit of £245,295 which was reached after the refinancing of *Saint Angus* (3). Without this action the underlying trading loss was £343,680. Freight rates and plant hire charges were too low to cover operating costs while unit costs at Bonawe were too high. *Saint Oran* (3) made a loss of £48,900 caused by poor trading on the open market and the group returned a Retained Loss of £56,556, which was carried forward.

The managed and owned fleet was small, although the company had supplied crews to Liverpool based Coe Metcalf Ltd from 1984 to 1992. For some time the company had examined the possibility of selling 228 Clyde Street. The building was sold for £272,500 during 1993 and the company moved into offices at 36 Washington Street. The company's registered office was changed at this time to Craigmaddie Office at the Struthers' family residence, Craigmaddie, Milngavie and in 1995 another move brought them to offices at 16 Robertson Street within the Clydeport Authority's building.

During 1992 the crewing contract with Coe Metcalf Ltd ended and seagoing staff employed by Gardners shrank from 235 to 132. Even with the sale of 228 Clyde Street the group reported retained losses. Bonawe Quarry had seen a reduced demand for its products although other plant and construction operations had seen increased work from contracts. £400,000 was set aside to replace plant and vehicles due to high maintenance costs and on contracting the company had to diversify from road surfacing to include excavation and road widening.

On 24 August 1994, J. & A. Gardner & Co Ltd's share capital was increased to 200,000 ordinary £1 shares following the creation of 107,986 shares. At an Extraordinary General Meeting held the same day a Special Resolution was passed to allow the Board to issue shares 'on such terms and conditions as they may in their discretion think fit'. An immediate consequence was the sale of 3750 shares at £19 each to Philip Darwin, making Mr Darwin's investment in the company £75,000. Mr Darwin became a Director of J. & A. Gardner & Co Ltd with immediate effect for a term of three years. A close friend of Alastair Struthers and a great-great-grandson of Charles Darwin, Mr Darwin's other directorships included The Smaller Companies Investment Trust PLC, Lomond Underwriting PLC, IFG Group PLC and Stolt Nielsen SA.

Gardners were now turning the corner. Accounts for the year ending October 1994 showed a trading profit of £73,932, shipping profits were up 275% as a result of improved trading conditions and rebates from leasing rentals and quarry and plant hire profits rose by 7%. However, the following year losses were £29,499, due mainly to plant breakdowns at the quarry. 1996 saw a downturn in stone cargoes from Bonawe attributed to the demise of Strathclyde Regional Council. It was expected there would be a gap in orders until the authorities which replaced Strathclyde assessed their requirements. This resulted in the quarry competing for contracts against other suppliers which affected profitability. The accounts to October 1996 showed a group loss of £137,620 with the quarry trading well until the second half of the year when demand dropped following the local government reorganisation. Shipping made a profit of £461,075.

Annabel Struthers became a Director on 29 June 1995 and on 12 October 1995 Alastair Struthers reduced his shareholding in the company to 35,375 shares, which included his 13,113 non-beneficiary shares, by transferring 17,208 shares by equal division between his three daughters. A further 9,835 shares still in the name of the late Mrs E. M. Struthers were transferred on 23 October. 6,556 shares passed to Annabel Struthers and the balance of 3,279 to Alastair Struthers and William Stevens, acting as executors for the late Mrs E. M. Struthers. On the same day half the shares held separately by Mr Struthers as Accumulation and Maintenance for his children were also transferred, 8,445 to Annabel Struthers and one to Elizabeth Struthers. Mr Darwin left the Board at the end of his three-year term although he retained his shareholding in the company and since then the Board has remained unchanged.

In 2001 the company shareholding stood at:

Mr A. J. Struthers	28,800
Mrs E. P. Struthers	1,000
Miss S. M. Struthers	20,738
Miss A. J. Struthers	20,738
Miss E. L. Struthers	5,736
Mr P. W. Darwin	3,750
Mr A. J. Struthers & Mr W. B. Stevens (exec for Mrs E. M. Struthers deceased)	6,556
Mr A. J. Struthers (accumulation for children)	8,446

With difficult trading conditions continuing into the new millennium, the company was again faced with the prospect of downsizing its operations. In November 2000, the offices within the Clydeport Authority building were vacated and the company moved out to the Glasgow suburb of Milngavie to the Struthers family home at Craigmaddie. Prior to this move, both Roddy Bell and Alastair Tear left J. & A. Gardner & Co Ltd. Mr Tear moved to a new shipbroking venture, Gardner Morrison Tear Ltd, in which the Gardner company holds a 33.3% stake. A result of this move was that the company's office staff now comprised Sandy Struthers, Annabel Struthers and Malcolm Glen, along with Captain Leitch and Captain Cunningham (Master of the **Saint Kearan**) and Peter Robertson, the company's marine engineering superintendent.

Sadly in early 2001, Malcolm Glen died suddenly at home after suffering a heart attack, depriving Gardners of an employee who had had nearly forty years with the company and whose expertise would be difficult to replace.

Following the sale of the **Saint Kearan** (3) and **Saint Oran** in March and April 2001 respectively, the Gardner company now owns only the **Saint Brandan** which continues to operate in the South Atlantic. In order to remain in existence, the company is now considering changing from being a ship owner to providing consultancy and other services, for example ISM compliance, to other owners.

*The company's widespread presence in the western Scotland and Irish Sea trades meant that another fleet member was never far away should one vessel suffer a problem. Sadly **Saint Ronan** tended to be afflicted by engine problems and these two views show her being towed by **Saint Modan** beneath the Connel Bridge in Loch Etive. The ships would be making their way to Bonawe on the northern shore of the loch.*

(Company archives)

CARGOES, CUSTOMERS & CHARTERS

GRANITE, STONE & ROADMAKING

The effect that granite had on the company's fortunes cannot be understated, the Gardner family realising it themselves by using GRANITE as the company's telegraphic address. Until the 1950s it was the company's main cargo and any ship not having an immediate cargo was sent to Bonawe to load for Glasgow where they discharged at Custom House Quay, between Victoria Bridge and Jamaica Street Bridge. Gardners' early ships had a small superstructure to allow passage under the bridges before Custom House Quay and their funnels were hinged so they could be lowered thus reducing what today is referred to as their air draught (the height from the waterline to the top of the uppermost mast).

Custom House Quay was opened in 1852 and was Gardners' principal discharging berth until it closed in 1966. One of their main customers was the Glasgow Corporation Tramways Department who used granite setts to strengthen tramlines and a special line was laid into Custom House Quay so lowloaders could transport granite to the Department's Pollokshields works.

*The loading of granite at Bonawe quarry kept many of the company's vessels in employment. As noted above, discharge in Glasgow was generally at Custom House Quay and it is here that the **Saint Fergus** was photographed in 1964. The pristine condition of the ship suggests that this may have been her maiden voyage.* *(W Ralston Ltd)*

Granite was also loaded for numerous ports and quays in the Irish Sea and Western Isles. They included Lochboisdale (South Uist), Lochmaddy (North Uist), Salen (Mull), Port Ellen, Castlebay, Lismore and Craignure. With the increasing use of hot tar being preferred on the islands, Bonawe switched to producing Compomac – a cold tar coating of the stone. This allowed the mix to be spread cold two weeks after it had been made and was especially suited for isolated sites. ,

During the 1970s production at the quarries increased due to the demand for armour stone used in sea defences, mainly in Orkney and Shetland, especially for the breakwaters at Sullom Voe oil terminal. During this period **Saint Kentigern** (2) was the main quarry ship supported by **Saint Fergus** and **Saint Ronan** (2) although chartered tonnage was occasionally used.

During 1977 Gardners chartered **Marsa** for six months to load aggregates for Bunessan on the island of Mull. Customers were civil engineering companies working on projects around the Highlands and included Christiani & Neilsen, Charles Brand, Rush & Tompkins and Nutalls.

In 1978 **Saint Kentigern** (2) discharged a new tar processing plant at Bonawe and later shipped its predecessor to Dublin. **Saint Oran** (3) became the company's 'quarry ship' after the loss of **Saint Kentigern** although as early as 1980 the company noted a considerable swing from seaborne to road deliveries. In late 1982, **Saint Oran** was chartered by Curnow Shipping Ltd to load bitumen drums and stone chips for the Scilly Isles and was also chartered in 1991 to Rex Lewis Ltd for several stone cargoes to the Scilly Isles. **Saint Oran** remained the company's quarry ship and loaded dry or tar-coated stone at Bonawe for Mull, Islay, Coll, Tiree and Shetland. She also loaded associated plant equipment including lorries, tar spreaders, road rollers, etc as deck cargo for use in road construction.

*The diminutive **Marsa** was chartered by the company in 1977. She was originally **Vic 85**.*
(Roy Cressey collection)

As well as their own quarries, Gardner ships used to load at other quarries which included Carreg-y-llam, Llanddulas, and Penmaenmawr in North Wales where stone and limestone were loaded for west coast and continental ports. **Edgar Dorman** and **David Dorman** were chartered in 1986 by Tarmac Ltd to carry stone from Cairnryan to Faslane to be used in the construction of the new Trident submarine facilities at Faslane. This charter was repeated in 1987 and in 1988 they were chartered by Norwest Holst Ltd and loaded at Campbeltown.

In October 1998 the Struthers family sold a 50% holding in their operations at Bonawe to Ennstone Ltd which subsequently purchased the remaining 50% in mid-1999. Although they have withdrawn from being quarrymasters, the Struthers family still retains the mineral rights to Bonawe Quarry for which Ennstone Ltd pays them an annual royalty fee.

*The 1970s saw **Saint Kentigern** used as the main ship to load stone at Bonawe quarry. Her deck crane, fitted on runners, facilitated discharge at some of the more remote destinations which she served.*
(J K Byass)

COAL

Coal was the principle industrial and domestic fuel of the 19th and early 20th centuries. Ireland has few natural coal deposits and has relied largely on imported coal for its needs. Coal was loaded in ports in South Wales, through Lancashire and Cumberland to locations on the Clyde. Loading ports included Newport, Cardiff, Swansea, Garston, Partington, Birkenhead, Preston, Workington, Maryport, Silloth, Ardrossan and Ayr. Destinations were as numerous including Belfast, Londonderry, Newry, Bangor and Larne in Northern Ireland and Sligo, Dundalk and Dungarvan in the Republic. Return cargoes of pitwood used in the mines as supports for the tunnel ceilings were carried or scrap for the Scottish steel mills.

Coal destined for Stornoway, Port Ellen, Tobermory, Lochmaddy and Lochboisdale in the Western Isles often meant a call at Bonawe to load back for Glasgow. In the Western Isles coal was not only used for domestic purposes but also the whisky industry. Occasionally coal was loaded in South Wales for Cornish ports such as Hayle returning with stone for the Bristol Channel. In the 1990s **Saint Oran** (3) loaded coal in one-ton bags for Port Ellen, Tiree and Lismore.

The freight rate for coal has always been low. Before oil became predominant, coal was cheap but plentiful and it provided a cargo when the only option might have been a ballast passage. In the 1950s the rate varied anywhere between 7s 8d (37p) and 14s 4d (72p) per ton. In 1974 the rate from Garston to Newry for a cargo loaded by **Saint William** was £1 6s (£1.30) per ton compared with a barley cargo worth £5 per ton. In the late 1970s Gardners regularly used **Saint Colman**, **Saint Aidan** (2) or **Saint William** to load coal but because of the poor freight rate there was always a possibility of them not being available as the company looked for better cargoes. Because of the demand for coal during the winter of 1971/72, **Ben Veen** (486grt/65) and **Wegro** (IRL, 471grt/55) were voyage chartered to load cargoes for Ireland.

During the late 1960s and early 1970s coal was imported to Dundalk from Szczecin, Gdansk and Emden by **Saint William**, **Saint Angus** (2) and **Saint Brandan** (3). The number of UK loading ports declined until only Glasson Dock, Garston, Newport, Swansea and Cardiff on the west coast and Blyth in the north-east remained.

*Often used to carry cargoes of coal, **Saint Aidan** was photographed as she made her way along the Manchester Ship Canal on 10 July 1978.* *(John Slavin)*

Gardners shipped large quantities of coal to northern and southern Ireland. The importers were Joseph Fisher & Sons Limited of Newry and Warrenpoint, Charles Neil & Company Limited, Bangor, and Belfast-based Cawoods and Kellys. They also loaded for Larne, Coleraine, Moville and Londonderry. Gardners also had contracts to the south and west of Ireland with Heiton-Docherty of Dublin, O'Rourke and Lockington of Dundalk.

During the winter months, Gardners were able to arrange salt cargoes, which were used to grit roads in the Highland region. The ships loaded in Runcorn or Weston Point for Invergordon and from there they made a short ballast trip to Blyth where they would load a return coal cargo. The winters of 1981/82 and 1982/83 were particularly severe and resulted in an increased demand for salt and coal. A number of British and foreign ships were voyage-chartered to load salt at Weston Point.

Gardners' involvement in the Irish household coal trade ended in 1987. Cawoods had given verbal agreements for a year figure of 250,000 tons to be loaded in Garston where they operated the loading equipment. Cawoods also transported coal in containers by rail from Northumberland through Ellesmere Port which made a loss. In an attempt to reverse these losses Cawoods agreed to give Kellys the 250,000 tons promised to Gardners in return for an equivalent amount from Kelly's which in future was to be carried in containers through Ellesmere Port.

ALUMINA

British Aluminium Co Ltd opened an alumina smelter at Fort William to produce aluminium in 1929. One of the most important factors in producing aluminium is a cheap and plentiful supply of electricity. This is produced in Scotland by hydro generation. Each ton of finished aluminium requires between 16,000 to 18,000 units of electricity. About four tons of bauxite is required to produce two tons of alumina which results in one ton of finished aluminium.

Their first plant was opened at Foyers on Loch Ness in 1896 and at about the same time a facility in Larne was opened to process bauxite from the British Aluminium mine at Cargan near Ballymena. Eventually Larne became too small to satisfy the demand for aluminium and a new plant was built at Burntisland, Fife, to process imported bauxite because the Irish bauxite was found to be impure. A factory at Kinlochleven at the head of Loch Leven was opened in 1908 and in 1939 another plant was opened at Newport, Monmouthshire, to process bauxite and produce alumina which was sent to Fort William and Kinlochleven for processing into aluminium.

British Aluminium owned a small coaster, **Loch Etive** (237grt/10), which was a sister of **Saint Modan** (1). Gardners had regular work loading alumina, cryolite and American petroleum, or special coke, used in the carbon factory, to Fort William with return cargoes of refined aluminium for the North West rolling mills. One of the first cargoes carried by **Saint Bedan** (1) in 1936 was special coke from Glasgow and aluminium from Larne for Kristiansand and she returned with cryolite for Fort William and Kinlochleven. During World War 2, **Saint Kentigern** (1) and **Bonawe** (2) discharged cinders at Kinlochleven and Fort William, presumably to mix with coal to reduce fuel consumption. **Bonawe** could load a cargo of 100 tons of special coke which in 1942 was worth 19s 0d (95p) per ton or 98 tons of cinders. For a time during the war Irish bauxite was loaded for Glasgow, its importance to the process outweighing its impurity.

A time sheet for **Bonawe** gives an idea of the conditions during the post-war years. Arriving at Alexandra Dock, Newport, at 08.50 on 28 January 1946, she began loading the following day at 10.00am and finished at 12.45pm on 30 January. She sailed for Kinlochleven at 13.20hrs with 335 tons 5 cwt of alumina at 21s 3d (£1.06) per ton.

Aluminium-related cargoes declined during the 1950s and by the early 1960s it was rare to see seaborne cargoes arriving at Fort William. Expansion at Burntisland and the opening of a plant at Invergordon on the Cromarty Firth in 1968 along with the closure of Larne (1947), Foyers (1967) and Newport (1972) meant alumina from Invergordon was transported overland to Fort William and Kinlochleven. **Saint William** arrived at Kinlochleven with coal in February 1972, possibly the largest consignment to arrive there and the last cargoes carried for British Aluminum were finished aluminium from Invergordon in the early 1980s.

SILVERSAND

Silversand became a regular cargo for the company during the 1940s and was loaded at Loch Aline where the quarry was operated by the Glasgow company Charles Tennant & Co Ltd. It was used in the glass and chemical industries based around Manchester and Liverpool and was discharged at Garston and Runcorn. The trade continued after the war and Loch Aline's position in the Sound of Mull gave Gardners another southbound cargo for ships returning from the Western Isles. In the early 1970s, silversand and labradorite began to be imported from Hellvik for Colgate Palmolive Ltd using **Saint Angus** (2), **Saint Aidan** (2) and **Saint William**.

Loch Aline was a regular loading point for **Saint Fergus** and **Saint Ronan** (2) for Tilcon Ltd. In July 1972, **Saint William** loaded an export cargo for Bohus in Sweden for Elektrokemiska. This became a regular cargo with **Saint Bedan** (2) being the preferred ship and she was replaced after her loss by **Craigallian** and **Loch Awe**. Owing to a shortage of tonnage in 1983, several ships were voyage-chartered to load silversand at Loch Aline for Warrenpoint, Dublin, Ardrossan, Runcorn, and Liverpool, with another chartered the following year to load for Ardrossan and Runcorn. In December 1983 the facility at Loch Aline was sold to Tilcon Ltd and silversand cargoes carried by Gardner vessels declined.

Saint Bedan was a frequent sight in the Manchester Ship Canal and in the 1970s she was the preferred ship for loading silversand at the quarry in Loch Aline, a somewhat remote location just off the northern shore of the Sound of Mull.

(J K Byass)

ICI & CHEMICALS

After World War 2, Gardners' ships were chartered by Alginate Industries which had set up seaweed processing plants at Barcaldine and Girvan. Two types of seaweed were processed with the alginic acids extracted used in many processes including one which put the froth in the head of a pint of beer. **Saint Blane**, **Saint Kentigern** (1) and **Saint Rule**, which earned £1457 per month for a charter from April to October 1946, were favourites for the work although most of the post war fleet were chartered at one time or another.

ICI charters involved carrying explosives. Nobels Explosives Co Ltd was one of the companies which formed ICI in the mid-1940s and they operated a small coaster fleet to transport explosives to powder grounds and anchorages for transhipment. Charters usually began at Irvine and lasted for a week, two at the most, although **Saint Bedan** (1) went on charter in November 1956 and was not returned until September 1958. **Saint Kilda** achieved the best daily rate of all the ships used when she was chartered in 1956 for £130 per day. Coming off charter at Lisbon, she sailed to Casablanca and there loaded a return cargo of scrap for Ardrossan.

Saint Aidan (1) was chartered on nine occasions in 1958 while **Saint Angus** (1), **Saint Bedan** (1) and **Saint Rule** were chartered at rates varying between £77 10s (£77.50) and £90 per day. When **Saint Bedan** (1) was chartered in March 1965 her rate was £90 per day, the same as 1958. **Saint Oran** (3), **Saint Angus** (3) and **Saint Brandan** (4) were chartered during the 1980s for explosive cargoes. ICI charters were fixed by Genchem Ltd acting as shipbrokers for ICI.

Saint Modan (2) was chartered by Alginate from February 1973 to load bulk calcium chloride at Winnington for Girvan, Irvine or Barcaldine which required the fitting of five cargo tanks in her hold. **Saint Ronan** (2) was also converted so that she could deputise for **Saint Modan**. Both ships were displaced from the route when **Saint Kearan** (3) was completed in 1978. She occasionally loaded at Winnington for Lerwick for either Kühne & Nagel or B. W. Mud Ltd which purchased the cargoes for use in the oil industry.

During the recession of the early 1980s, **Saint Kearan** (3) traded around the UK, Scandinavia and the continent because there was not enough Alginate work. She loaded a variety of cargoes including drill and lubricating oil, transformer oil, drilling mud and the chemicals Distillate 600, BEX.2 and HPO100. The latter cargo was loaded at Old Kilpatrick for J. O. Buchanan which was eventually taken over by Carless Capel Ltd. In turn this company was taken over by the Spanish firm REPSOL which manufactured the same products as the Old Kilpatrick facility thus resulting in the latter's closure.

The 1960-built **Saint Modan** was modified to carry liquid calcium chloride from Winnington. This meant the fitting of tanks in her hold and a hose for discharging. This hose is visible beneath the aft derrick in this view of the ship passing Eastham at the start of a voyage northwards. *(J K Byass)*

In 1982 the volume of liquid cargo was proving too much for **Saint Kearan** (3) and the company considered buying or chartering another tanker depending on levels for the next two years. Those vessels available for charter were too big for Winnington and the purchase price for a 15-year-old German tanker of suitable size was some £300,000. This was considered too high and confirmation would be required that she could carry the liquids in question. In the event, no additional tanker was acquired although **Bragd** (NOR 1,594grt/74) was chartered in May 1983 for a single cargo of bulk calcium chloride from Eastham to Peterhead and Lerwick.

Saint Kearan is seen at Winnington as she began to load cargo on 28 December 1996. Just visible in the left background is the top of the Anderton Lift, built to transport small boats between the higher level of the Trent & Mersey Canal and the lower level of the Weaver Navigation. *(Bernard McCall)*

Saint Kearan was joined by **Saint Oran** (3) in 1981 and the majority of **Saint Kearan**'s cargoes were carried for Alginate which now trades as Kelco Ltd. During 1999, a question mark arose over the commercial future of the River Weaver after cargoes began to be transported by road tanker to either Eastham or Liverpool for onward sea carriage. The British Waterways Board which maintains the Weaver would like to see the river remain open to commercial vessels and an attempt is being made to resolve the situation. The Barcaldine plant closed during 1997 and cargoes for Peterhead and Aberdeen were loaded for the Brunner Mond Ltd account. Following the sale of **Saint Kearan**, cargoes originating at Winnington are now carried by vessels chartered on a voyage basis.

INDIVISIBLE LOADS

Henry Abram & Sons Ltd. was formed in 1927 to handle ship deliveries and heavy abnormal loads and Gardners became associated with them before World War 2, **Saint Angus** (1) carrying machinery and gear casings from Glasgow to Portsmouth in February 1939. Abram cargoes increased during the 1960s which coincided with a downturn in ICI charters and this involved heavy machinery for power stations such as Hinkley Point, Wylfa and Kingsnorth. Later, another regular cargo was twin 4" gun mountings to naval shipyards which were usually loaded at Scotstoun. As all the associated equipment below the mounting rested on the hold floor the turret was above the hatch coamings. Once in place carpenters went aboard to secure the mountings by fitting wooden beams. The regular ship for this work was **Saint Brandan** (3), which loaded for Belfast, Portsmouth, Rosyth, Birkenhead, Southampton, Hebburn-on-Tyne, Barrow and Yarrow's berth on the Clyde.

During 1963, **Saint Aidan** (2) loaded Stulcken derricks at Hamburg for Charles Connell at Scotstoun on the Clyde while **Saint Brandan** (3) loaded six Euclid dumper trucks in Cardiff for Holyhead returning in February 1964 to load the same trucks back to Cardiff. Later **Saint Angus** (2) and **Saint Bedan** (2) found regular Abram-related work, **Saint Angus** being chartered for five months in 1971 at £90 per day. The 1970s saw the beginning of oil exploration around the UK coast which resulted in better charter rates. **Saint Bedan** was hired at £400 per day for five weeks in November 1973 to supply rig legs to a jack up rig lying in the Gareloch. The rig's crane discharged the cargo and **Saint Bedan** was required to remain in a constant position alongside during unloading. In December 1973, **Saint William** was fixed for a heavy lift cargo which was cancelled when it was found she was too large for the discharge port and Gardners received £300 compensation from Abrams. In 1974, **Saint Bedan** and **Saint William** were both hired to transport ship's propellers between Scott Lithgow's yard and James Watt Dock, Greenock.

Saint Bedan *was regularly chartered on behalf of Henry Abram & Sons Ltd who specialised in the carriage of abnormal loads. Here she is seen at Birkenhead loading propellers manufactured at the works of Stone Manganese Ltd, adjacent to the docks.*
(Company archives)

Gardners loaded large and awkward cargoes for other companies and in the 1960s and 1970s their ships were often fixed with the Glasgow shipping and forwarding agents Davidson, Park & Speed Ltd. Transformers and heavy machinery were usually loaded in Glasgow for the Mersey, Rosyth and Tilbury. In 1961, **Saint Brandan** (3) sailed from the Tyne with machinery for Viana do Castelo, Portugal. In June 1974, **Saint William** loaded two whisky stills in Glasgow for Cork for which Gardners received £3,000. In 1962, **Saint Aidan** (2) loaded two boilers in Glasgow for Greenock and later loaded machinery in Greenock for Cadiz.

Saint Colman is seen at Port Glasgow discharging two items of heavy machinery which would ultimately be installed in a ship being constructed in the local Scott Lithgow shipyard. The information "panel" rigged at the side of the machinery informs us that it was made by Babcock for J G Kincaid Co Ltd.
(Company archives)

The first of the Wivenhoe-built ships, **Saint Kentigern**, leaves Ardrossan with a deck cargo of construction equipment.
(Jack W Boyd)

Propellers and hatch covers for new ships being constructed in numerous shipyards provided work for **Saint Bedan** (2) and **Saint Angus** (2) in the 1970s and they discharged these at Gothenburg, Uddevalla, Copenhagen and Wallsend. In 1969 **Saint Aidan** (2) loaded a combine harvester and machinery in Ardrossan for Dublin while the following year **Saint Angus** (3) loaded two hovercraft in Grimsby for Southampton and Greenock. The small ships also played their part, **Saint Ronan** (2) transhipping two suckers to **Armonia** (GRC, 9443grt/61) at the Tail of the Bank in 1970.

The roll-on/roll-off capability of the Wivenhoe-built ships added a new dimension to what Gardners were able to offer their customers. During 1977 **Saint Brandan** (4) loaded dumper trucks for Sullom Voe and Agadir on behalf of Frank Armitt Ltd as well as plant machinery for Lochboisdale, South Uist. **Saint Kentigern** (2) meanwhile loaded a land rig for Shapinsay on behalf of Peckston Shipping Ltd and also a crane to Loch Carnan for Gardners' own use.

Between 1978 and 1983 **Saint Brandan** (4) loaded several straddle carriers for handling containers. The charterer was again Frank Armitt Ltd and these were loaded in Manchester, Southampton, Antwerp and Le Havre. **Saint Angus** loaded such cargoes during 1982 and 1983 because **Saint Brandan** was on charter in the Falklands.

On 2 October 1981, **Saint Angus** sailed from Milford Haven with an Abram heavy lift cargo for Methil which was lost overboard in bad weather. She returned to Milford Haven and later loaded contractors' plant for Fleetwood. At the end of 1981 she loaded a helipad and machinery for Kishorn. From 1982 to 1986, **Saint Brandan**, **Saint Angus** and **Saint Oran** were often chartered to transport submarine rings from the Clyde to Barrow on behalf of Abram's, **Saint Oran** loading one ring in Leith for Glasgow in May 1986. In September 1984, **Saint Oran** loaded her first heavy lift cargo which was a water-processing module from Gloucester to Avonmouth for Bethyll Gwyn Ltd. In 1997 she loaded the hulls of two coastal training craft, **Raider** and **Tracker**, which had been built at Falmouth by Kingfisher Ltd, for Troon where they were fitted out by Ailsa Perth Shipbuilders Ltd for the Royal Navy.

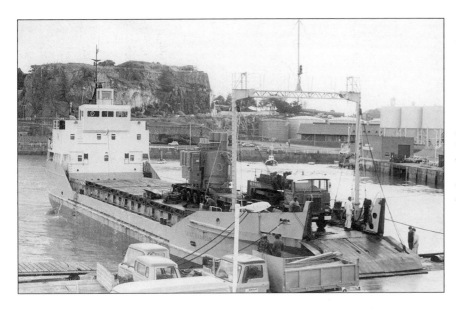

*Many of the heavy loads handled by Gardner ships were pieces of power station equipment. **Saint Brandan** visited St Helier, Jersey, to discharge two transformers for the local power station on 27 October 1984.* *(Dave Hocquard)*

Saint Angus was also used regularly for such loads. She was photographed at Douglas, Isle of Man, on 7 March 1989 when delivering equipment for a new power station being built on the island at Pulrose.

(Alan Kelly - Mannin Postcards)

Another island to receive power station equipment was Skye. On this occasion in June 1978, it was **Saint Kentigern** which was used and she is seen at the small jetty at Broadford.

(Alistair MacDonald)

A completely different kind of heavy lift is shown here. On 26 January 1992, **Saint Angus** was a rare arrival in Bristol's Cumberland Basin where she loaded machinery and equipment manufactured locally to be installed on a dredger being built near Rotterdam.

(Cedric Catt)

As noted on the previous page, Gardner vessels were used in the late 1970s and early 1980s to convey straddle carriers used in handling containers. With **Saint Brandan** at work in the Falklands, **Saint Angus** was used towards the end of this period and she was photographed passing Cadishead on her way down the Manchester Ship Canal in June 1983.

(John Slavin)

Saint Brandan conveys two straddle carriers of differing dimensions as she enters the Mersey from the Manchester Ship Canal at Eastham.

(J K Byass)

OIL EXPLORATION AND CIVIL ENGINEERING

Gardners became involved in oil exploration and related construction work during 1974 when **Saint Kentigern** (2) was hired by William Tawse Ltd to work in the Kishorn and Kyle area at £600 per day. This was twice the rate she had earned for recent charter to Irish Sea Ferries Ltd and in 1976 Sea Platforms (Scotland) Ltd took her on a three month charter worth £750 per day working between Portavadie and Ardrossan. Later they chartered both her and **Saint Ronan** (2) to attend pontoon modules at Dumbarton with **Saint Ronan** earning £500 for one day's work and **Saint Kentigern** £3,000 for four days. In August and September 1976, Kramo Montage UK Ltd hired **Saint Kentigern** for more oil-related work.

Various civil engineering groups chartered **Saint Kentigern** while oil-rig yards were being built on the west coast of Scotland and she was a suitable vessel because of her unusual bow design and ramp facility. Some new coastal sites had no proper access and the civil engineers used the *BUND* method to allow the vessel to land heavy earth moving plant ashore. A tracked bulldozer would build up a raised roadway of earth and stone and extend it from the shoreline seawards until it was out to the half tide mark or further. Near high water the vessel would approach the seaward end of the bund, placing the bow against the end of the bund and the bow ramps were lowered onto the bund allowing the vehicles or plant to drive ashore. This was a temporary but nevertheless useful way of landing heavy plant at a virgin site and the flood tide washed away part of the bund as it flooded, the roadway sank slightly with tracked vehicles transiting, but with additional earth moving equipment landed each time it became easier to rebuild and strengthen the bund for the vessel's arrival at the next high water. This system was used at Loch Kishorn, Arnish, Stornoway, Portavadie and other coastal sites.

*The **Saint Kentigern** is seen discharging contractors' equipment at Loch Kishorn in 1974.* (Alistair MacDonald)

What were called the 'Bonawe Beams' were also used on the bunds. These were beams designed by Mr William Leitch, Gardner's Superintendent Engineer, and allowed side loading of heavy tracked cranes and machines onto the hatches of the conventional coasters before any of the vessels had heavy Macgregor steel hatch covers fitted. The beams could only be used when the height of the tide allowed the hatch coamings to be a certain height above the quay wall. Two parallel ramps were positioned from the quayside onto the hatch coaming, with two parallel ramps extending right across the hatch athwartships and beyond the outward hatch coaming. The ramps were designed in such a way that as the weight of the plant transferred from the shore to the vessel it tracked aboard the ramps locked to make a rigid bridge being held together by large heavy pins and a locking arrangement. The shore beams were then loaded aboard the vessel and the heavylift and all the beams were then secured for sea.

*Stormy weather lies ahead but the deck cargo of **Saint Kentigern** is lit by bright sunlight as she makes her way to Arnish with construction equipment in 1974.*

(Joe McGavock)

In 1975, Gardners were the agents for **Wib**, **Wis** (both 199grt/70) and **Wopper** (260grt/68) owned by Eggar Forrester Ltd and which had been chartered to work from Ardrossan to Portavadie and Loch Kishorn by Sea Platforms Ltd. Glenlight Ltd later chartered the three ships and two others, **Wilks** (199grt/69) and **Wiggs** (199grt/70), to supply sand and aggregates to the Howard Doris yard at Loch Kishorn. Glenlight later purchased them to replace their ageing fleet of Clyde puffers. Irishenco, working at Portavadie, had equipment completed at Ardrossan, which was then towed to Portavadie. The agent at Ardrossan was R. L. Alpine & Co, which was jointly owned by Gardners and Glenlight.

On 22 July 1977, the Epirotiki S. S. Co vessel **Odysseus** (CYP, 4,307grt/37) arrived in the Clyde for lay up after serving as an accommodation ship for oil rig workers in Loch Kishorn. Gardners were the ship's agents for the next two years until she was sold for demolition and broken up at Faslane by Shipbreaking Industries Ltd. On two occasions in 1978, **Saint Kentigern** (2) was used as a service vessel to the jack-up rig **Zephyr 1** (DNK, 4778grt/73) lying in Lamlash Bay, Arran. This work involved taking out equipment and supplies and returning with empty gas bottles, scrap and slop oil.

With the development of ferry services to the Western Isles new linkspans to take the ferries' stern and bow ramps were required at sites on the mainland and the Western Isles. Linkspans are steel structures with the inner, or shore end, hinged to allow them to be raised and lowered while a wire or hydraulic hoist controls the seaward end allowing height adjustment to suit the height of the ferry's vehicle ramp. Linkspans designed by Crouch & Hogg Ltd were carried to Lochboisdale and Wemyss Bay and those at Lochmaddy, Uig and Tarbert (Harris) were built by Sir William Arrol Ltd.

OTHER CUSTOMERS & CARGOES

Colin McPhail & Co was another 'puffer' company to use Gardners' ships and up to the 1960s Gardners carried seaweed from Kilkieran, County Mayo, for McPhails to a collecting station at Kames. From there it was taken to Barcaldine for processing by Alginate Industries Ltd. A cheap and plentiful cargo, the rate was only 33s 11d (£1.69) per ton in 1954.

David MacBrayne entered shipping in 1849 and the name MacBrayne is synonymous with the Western Isles. Through a series of mergers the company is still in existence as Caledonian MacBrayne Ltd which maintains present day ferry services throughout the region. Alastair Struthers is also a former Chairman and Board member of Caledonian MacBrayne Ltd. MacBraynes chartered several of Gardners' ships during and immediately after World War 2 for short periods. These included **Saint Bedan** (1), **Bonawe** (2), **Saint Rule**, **Saint Angus** (1), **Saint Kentigern** (1), **Ardachy** and **Ardchattan** which were all taken on charter for varying lengths of time. As late as 1973 **Saint Ronan** (2) was chartered by Caledonian MacBrayne Ltd for three months work around Kyle, Raasay and Stornoway. In 1974, **Saint Kentigern** (2) took hay, petrol and foodstuffs to Coll, Tiree and Barra after the regular ferry had become stormbound.

Another company to use Gardner's during the war was Burns & Laird Ltd which operated passenger and cargo services between north-west England and Ireland. **Saint Bedan** (1) was chartered from November 1943 for four months earning the company £1,788 7s (£1,788.35). **Saint Kentigern** (1) was chartered twice in 1944 and **Saint Aidan** (1) was hired from December 1944 until March 1945 and again in November for three months at £323 11s (£323.55) per day. Burns & Laird charters continued for some time after the war but like other work dwindled and eventually disappeared with the advent of containerisation and modern ferries.

*The 1941-built **Saint Rule** was one of the Gardner ships chartered by David MacBrayne during and after World War 2 to assist with cargo work in western Scotland.*

(John Clarkson)

The Liverpool & Glasgow Salvage Association hired **Bonawe** (2) for seven days in August 1940 and in November 1942 Clyde Shipping Co Ltd chartered her for four months. In 1946 and 1947 **Saint Angus** (1) was chartered by Cunard on three separate occasions, one short term the other two for six months. Other notable companies to use Gardners included the Glasgow shipbrokers McLarens, Belfast S. S. Co Ltd which took **Saint Aidan** (1) on a ten-day charter in January 1949 and the Liverpool Salvage Association which used **Saint Rule** for seven days in the Clyde during October 1964 alongside **Vivanita**.

From the 1930s until the 1950s Gardners were involved in the Channel Island's early season fruit and vegetable trade. Before the war **Saint Angus** (1) and **Saint Bedan** (1) worked in the area earning £450 and £500 per month respectively. Both ships returned in 1953 when **Saint Bedan** was chartered to John S. Sellars & Co while **Saint Angus** made several visits to northern French ports. In 1937 the same ships were chartered to S.C.W.S Ltd (Scottish Co-operative Wholesale Society), **Saint Angus** from March to August, losing £243 as a result of being off hire for thirteen days in April and **Saint Bedan** from September 1937 until December 1938.

During World War 2, Gardners' ships sailed under Government orders and loaded cargoes which they would not have done in normal circumstances. Between them, **Saint Angus**, **Saint Aidan**, **Saint Bedan** and **Saint Rule** loaded a variety of cargoes for the Ministry of Food which included peanuts, tea, dried fruit, seed cake and salted herring from Shetland to Germany with a return cargo of empty boxes and ice. After the war, **Saint Angus** loaded six individual ammunition cargoes in Glasgow for Llanelli, which were spread over four months from December 1945 to March 1946.

The steel plants in South Wales and north-west England created a demand for raw materials. Cargoes of finished products were also available. Pig iron was loaded in the 1940s and 1950s at Millom in Cumbria, Liverpool or Swansea while steel sheets were loaded at Port Talbot for the Clyde and steel rails for Garston. Ships like **Saint Kentigern** (1) were well suited for small ports and quays and she carried bricks to Haulbowline, salt to Stornoway, firebricks to Llanelli and in October 1948 she loaded hut sections for Ardrishaig. She and **Bonawe** (2) loaded a number of cotton cargoes between 1947 and 1950 in Liverpool for Paisley while in July 1948 **Saint Angus** (1) discharged 299 tons of linseed at Gloucester.

A note appears in the cargo book of **Bonawe** (2) saying that the Master received a payment of £1 after discharging boiler equipment at Avonmouth which was presumably due to extra work in the loading and unloading the cargo. During the 1950s the older steamers tended to load dirty cargoes such as coal, granite, sand, scrap and phosphates that would not require much hold cleaning. That said, in 1951 **Saint Kearan** (2) loaded in Bideford grain destined for the Caol Ila distillery on Islay which was discharged at Port Ellen. In 1961 **Saint Angus** (1) loaded 943 tons of chocolate for Cadburys over three cargoes which were carried from Cork to Bristol at 25s (£1.25) per ton. Ten years later **Saint Bridget** loaded chocolate crumbs in Cork for Sharpness for a freight of £750.

Cargo book entries for the 1950s show Gardner's loaded cargoes which included pig iron, oats, fish meal, herring oil in barrels, empty herring barrels, potatoes, cement, milk, millet, scrap, bricks, pitch, salt, soda ash, fertiliser and cement clinker. Entries for the 1960s and 1970s saw the company carrying bananas, jute, asbestos pipes, steel coils, French wheat, animal feed, dolomite, woodchips, pyrites and abnormal loads. The trading area expanded from the Irish Sea to the Baltic, Northern Europe and the Mediterranean. Ports visited included Rouen, Kenitra, Malaga, Seville, Bilbao, Figueira, Bordeaux, Blaye and Leixoes. In January 1987, **Saint Oran** (3) arrived at Silloth with palletised cement from Aberdeen, the first time for many years that a company ship had visited Silloth where once it was commonplace.

Gardners entered the Scandinavian timber trade in 1958 when **Saint Kilda** loaded two cargoes at Mariestad and Oskarshamn for Hull and Liverpool, Manchester and Preston. She returned to the Baltic in 1959 and 1960, usually loading a positioning cargo of coal on the east coast of England. In 1960 she earned £6,100 for two timber cargoes in one month compared to seven cargoes, four coal and three sand, in August worth £4,117. **Saint Brandan** (3) loaded her first timber cargo in 1960 and **Saint Kilda** her last cargo in 1961 when she loaded timber worth £4,057 at Väsa for Preston.

Although the carriage of timber was not a regular work it was profitable compared to other cargoes. It provided perhaps only three or four cargoes a year, usually shared between Saint Brandan (3) and Saint Aidan (2), which in 1964 loaded three cargoes worth £14,677. Saint Aidan was the last ship to be involved in the trade when she loaded wood chips at Larvik for Barrow in 1972. On arrival at Barrow she was strikebound for four weeks. Sadly the date and location of this photograph of Saint Kilda about to discharge cargo are unknown.

(Company archives)

*By contrast we know that **Saint Brandan** was discharging her cargo of timber at Southampton on a rather dull September day in 1965.*

(Rodney Agutter)

*In these days of packaged and pre-slung timber, we tend to forget how labour-intensive timber cargoes were thirty years ago. There are no less than twelve stevedores handling individual planks as deck cargo on **Saint Brandan**.*

(Company archives)

As well as acting as agents for their own ships in the Clyde Gardners also acted for other owners and in the 1970s they were agents for ships discharging grain at Spillers' mills in Glasgow. In 1985 and 1986, the company was agent for Fred Olsen's **Black Prince** (NOR, 9,499gt/66) which visited the Clyde as part of a round-UK cruise programme visiting National Trust properties. Other ships represented range from the Port Glasgow-built **Sugar Producer** (13,436grt/68) during her sale in October 1979, when she was renamed **Cape Avanti Due,** to **Stridence** (BHS, 699gt/83) which discharged grain during May 1997 at King George V Dock.

SHIPOWNERS: 1876 TO 2001

1876 - 1918 : THE FIRST STEAMSHIPS

James Gardner's first vessel, **Helen MacGregor**, was a steamship of 64 gross tons measuring 65.5 feet in length and powered by a 20-hp engine. Completed in August 1876 by William Swan & Son at their Maryhill yard, she carried granite from Ballachulish to Glasgow and returned with cargoes for the remote settlements near and around Loch Leven. In May 1877, Swans completed another steamer, **Rob Roy**, which was similar in size to **Helen MacGregor**. James Gardner took a mortgage of £1410 plus interest of 10% with the builders to pay for her construction which was discharged in November 1878. A further two mortgages were taken out on the vessel and these were discharged before her sale to Isle of Man owners in May 1883.

Road construction is a seasonal business which relies on good weather and during the winter months the two ships worked in the Irish household coal trade where they were suited for small ports such as Letterkenny and Dungarvan. In 1892 the thirty-two year old **Cuirassier** was purchased by Duncan MacGregor Gardner. She was built to carry china clay from Poole to the River Severn and had a sliding keel, drawn up while sailing on waterways, to help her stability while at sea. Within two years she was lost in 1894 near Cumbrae Lighthouse and to replace her the four-year-old **Norman** was bought from Glasgow owners. Measuring 136 feet she was a much larger vessel than had been previously owned. In the same year another steamer, **Aston**, was bought from Welsh owners. **Norman** was sold in May 1897 to French owners, trading for another seventeen years before her loss in 1914.

In 1897 **Helen MacGregor** was lost with her four crew which included Captain McDougall who had survived the sinking of **Cuirassier** in 1894. The vessel had been sold to Duncan MacGregor Gardner the previous year to replace **Cuirassier**. She disappeared while on passage from Glasgow to Salen, Mull, with a cargo of coal. She sailed from Glasgow via the Crinan Canal, passing through the canal on 26 November, having spent the previous night at Ardrishaig. By the time of her last sighting, as she passed through the Sound of Luing and past Fladda, the wind had increased to gale force. It was presumed she sank somewhere near the southwest tip of the Isle of Kerrera as the body of a seaman and lifebelt came ashore at the southern end of the island on 30 November. There was also some wreckage, hatchcovers and boat parts, as well as a name board bearing part of the name **Helen Mac**. Another body, with papers including an old bill of lading for **Helen MacGregor**, was found on the western end of the island. A Board of Trade inquiry held the following March established that the vessel had undergone various repairs and a large sum of money had been spent which should have made the vessel sound. One witness told the inquiry he had noticed three to four inches of water lying in her bilges as she passed through the Crinan Canal. This could be due to her lying the previous evening for twelve hours without her pumps working which was not unusual for a vessel of her age.

Helen MacGregor's replacement came from the same French owners who had bought **Norman** the previous year. and she was renamed **Wharfinger**. In December 1900, **Wharfinger** grounded in Loch Indaal, Islay, after her anchor chains parted and it was estimated that it would cost £200 to dig a trench to refloat her. Salvage work began on 9 January 1901 and she remained there until the end of March when she sailed for Bonawe.

On the morning of 31 January 1903, **Aston** was outward from Glasgow with coal for Bonawe, when she was in collision near the entrance to the Great Harbour, Greenock, with the steam tug **Neptune** (165grt/1893). **Aston** was beached at Garvel Point and was not refloated until 9 February and the next day was slipped at Bowling for survey. Not worth repairing she was sold for breaking up later that year.

To replace **Aston**, a brand new steamer was ordered from Scott & Sons, Bowling. She was launched on 22 October 1903 as **Bonawe** (1). Of 242 gross tons and fitted with an 260 ihp engine built by Fisher & Co, Paisley, she was the first of twenty ships to be built at Bowling for Gardners. As well as building ships for Gardners, Scotts carried out numerous repairs and slippings for Gardners until the yard closed in the late 1970s. In October 1906, J. & A. Gardner & Co Ltd was created and the first ship built for the new company was completed by Scotts the following March. Named **Ardchattan** she was slightly larger than **Bonawe** and her engine was a more powerful 300-ihp unit.

The opportunity was taken in 1908 to acquire a second-hand coaster that had been recently declared a constructive total loss. Built in 1904 by Scotts as **Radium** for Young & Gillespie's British Coasting S. S. Co Ltd, she had struck a rock half a mile west of Doherty Rock on 30 May 1907 when in ballast from Ramelton for Glasgow. Eventually brought into Malin Harbour, she was abandoned to her underwriters and Gardners purchased her in January 1908, renaming her **Ardachy**.

In 1910 another steamship entered service and started a naming system that lasts to the present day. **Saint Modan** (1) was launched at Bowling on 13 January and was a single hold vessel measuring 122 feet. Before she was delivered in February, **Wharfinger** had foundered in the Sound of Mull on a voyage from Glasgow to Carbost, Skye, on 21 January 1911, with coal. Fortunately all six of her crew were saved. In 1911 an order was placed with Scotts for a sister to **Saint Modan** which was completed in December 1911 as **Saint Oran** (1).

The company remained unaffected by World War 1 until 1917 when **Bonawe** became the company's first war loss. On a voyage from Ayr to Larne with coal, she sank after colliding with H. M. patrol vessel **Iolaire** on 7 June, 1.5 miles north-east of Point Corrie, Isle of Arran. Captain Hannah and his six crew all survived.

In August 1917, the first of six raised quarterdeck steamers was delivered from Scotts. **Saint Barchan** (1) was a two hatch steamer built on a 141.5' hull and she, and her sisters, had a gross tonnage of 360-370 tons. Previously Scotts had built single hatch, short raised quarterdeck 120-130' steamers for Gardners. Unfortunately **Saint Barchan** was sunk with the loss of all eight crew on 21 October 1918 four miles from St. John's Point, County Down, by the German submarine **UB94**. She was on passage from Ayr to Dublin with coal and was the last vessel sunk in British waters during World War 1, Germany ordering all her submarines back to German ports the following day.

*It is clearly a winter's day which finds **Ardchattan** and **Saint Oran** (2) at Custom House Quay in Glasgow. The date is thought to be the mid-1940s.*

(Company archives)

1920 - 1939 : SURVIVING THE SLUMP AND QUIET EXPANSION

Following the end of World War 1, Gardners took delivery of another four ships from Scotts. **Saint Enoch** (1) was completed in November 1918, **Saint Barchan** (2) and **Bonawe** (2) in October and December 1919 and **Saint Aidan** (1) in 1920. Because of the very poor trading conditions which existed throughout the 1920s only another three ships were added to the fleet during the 1920s, two being replacements for casualties. On the night of 30 December 1920, **Saint Oran** sank after colliding with the steamer **Eveleen** (498grt/20) between Ailsa Craig and Turnberry. Commanded by Captain Mitchell, she was on passage from Troon to Larne with coal.

Saint Enoch proved to be a long-serving member of the Gardner fleet. Built in 1918, she traded until her eventual sale for scrap after grounding off the coast of Northern Ireland in 1955.

(J K Byass)

While on a voyage from Barry to Glasgow with cement, **Saint Barchan** went ashore at Iron Rock Ledge, Arran, on 12 March 1923. Due to the weather a lifeboat was unable to get alongside and her crew spent five hours in their boat before landing at Blackwaterfoot, Arran. Her master boarded the next day and found that the engineroom was holed and her propeller blades broken. A salvage crew and diver boarded her on 21 March and using pumps were able to dry the ship's holds within an hour. Her engineroom showed little damage and the salvage team was able to discharge fifty tons of cargo. On 3 April she was shifted further inshore to allow further discharge of the cargo and having been refloated the following day she was towed to Lamlash, sailing under tow on 6 April for repairs at Bowling.

Scotts delivered **Saint Oran** (2) in July 1923 which was similar in size to **Saint Oran** (1) and **Saint Modan** (1). In November 1924 they completed **Saint Brandan** (1) which was the last in the series of raised threequarterdeck steamers which had begun with **Saint Barchan** (1). **Saint Brandan** was another ship with a short career, being lost in 1928. She sailed from Skye for Glasgow on Friday 19 October with 200 tons of barley, although a report in the *Daily Telegraph* stated she also carried whisky worth £8,000. Off the Cairns of Coll she ran into a severe south-westerly storm and grounded North of the Rubha Mor peninsula, North West Coll. Captain Dougal MacDonald and nine crew abandoned **Saint Brandan** in two ship's boats and spent three hours trying to row to the shore before they were picked up by the Fleetwood trawler **City of York** (202grt/04). **Saint Brandan** had stranded with her midships caught between two rocks and during the night of 19/20 she was exposed to the storm. Her hull hammered continuously on the rocks and opened out at the sternpost and she lost her bottom. On 20 October she was reported to have overturned and sunk in about nine to ten fathoms of water. **Bonawe** arrived in the area on 22 October and reported there was no trace of the wreck.

The 1919-built **Saint Barchan** underwent various modifications during her career. Some people have suggested that the photograph on the left depicts the original **Saint Barchan** built in 1917 but this is not correct. This ship had been lost by 1918 so it is unlikely that there are any photographs of her. In fact, we see the 1919 **Saint Barchan** arriving at Preston, probably in the 1920s, in what was her original condition.

(World Ship Photo Library)

Saint Barchan was in a collision in the Manchester Ship Canal in 1932 and it may have been after that that alterations were made. Readers will be able to see many differences, but note the altered wheelhouse and bridge wings, only two washports abreast No. 2 hatch, mizzen mast removed, boatdeck altered. Both views should be compared to that on page 66.

(World Ship Photo Library)

To replace **Saint Brandan** (1), a new ship was ordered from Scott & Sons and was completed in July 1929 as **Saint Kearan** (1). Twelve months later, **Saint Brandan**'s name was revived for another ship completed by Scotts in July 1930. On 6 April 1932, **Saint Barchan** collided with the Norwegian tanker **Morgenen** (7093grt/30) in the Manchester Ship Canal and the subsequent court case found in favour of the Norwegians, holding the **Saint Barchan** to blame for the collision.

Like her earlier namesake, **Saint Brandan** (2) had a short life, being lost on 21 June 1935, south-east of Cape Barfleur. Commanded by Captain Alexander Brown, she grounded in thick fog while on a voyage from Port Talbot to Rouen with coal. Refloated the following day she sank while under tow five miles from Cherbourg. Her place in the fleet was taken by **Princetown**, bought from Dublin owners for £3,100 and renamed **Saint Conan** (1).

BONAWE FERRY

When John and Alexander Gardner took the lease on Bonawe Quarry, they also acquired possession of the Bonawe ferry crossing. Dating back to time immemorial it was a foot crossing maintained by rowing boats which were superseded by motor launches and crossed a strip of water 370 yards wide. Situated where the old west and north drove roads converged, Bonawe, or Bunaw or Bun Atha, means Mouth of the River Awe and the crossing was well used by people from such places as Glen Etive in the northeast and Appin in the west. Following the 1745 Rebellion, it was one of many roads known as Wade Roads after the English General Wade who improved access to the Highlands, no doubt to put down quickly any further uprisings rather than to help trading conditions. The opening of the ironworks on the south side of the loch in the mid-eighteenth century, followed by the quarry in the 1880s on the north bank, helped the ferry's importance. Following the opening of the quarry, the northern approach road was improved. In the late 1800s three rowing boats, two small and one large, maintained the crossing. The larger boat had a capacity for a load of three tons and was not suited to carrying motor cars. It was not until shortly before World War 1 that a larger boat capable of carrying ten tons was put into service. In 1936, J. & A. Gardner & Co Ltd proposed the upgrading of the crossing by the introduction of a vehicular ferry, so competing with the fixed crossing at Connel Bridge operated by the London, Midland & Scottish Railway Co Ltd.

The bridge at Connel had been built in the 1890s and trains carried motor cars after their petrol tanks had been emptied, their passengers still using the ferry. Prior to World War 1, the track over the bridge, next to the railway, became a toll bridge which could be used by vehicles and pedestrians when no trains were expected.

The proposal was successful and the company widened the slips at Bonawe to twenty-five feet and extended the slip at Taynuilt by eighteen feet. Argyll County Council upgraded the roads to the north and south of the ferry to allow motor vehicles access to the improved crossing. An order was placed with H. McLean & Sons Ltd, Renfrew, for a small vehicle ferry fitted with a turntable and capable of carrying four cars or a small bus, or a ten-ton lorry. A beam loading vessel she was similar to the ferries on other Scottish services and was under contract to the Post Office to carry mail to Bonawe. Company records show that the building contract required the vessel to be delivered no later than 30 March 1937.

The new ferry was named **Deirdre**, after the Gaelic heroine who fled from Ulster to the Glen Etive area. After **Deirdre** entered service the Connel Bridge fare was reduced to about 5s (25p) per vehicle, half the price it had previously been. During World War 2, **Deirdre** was requisitioned for service with the Government and the service was again maintained by small boats until **Deirdre** was returned at the end of the war. There were now several hundred workers at the quarry giving the ferry a guaranteed customer base and income.

By 1956, **Deirdre** was due for replacement and a new ferry was ordered from James Noble (Fraserburgh) Ltd. Built of wood and with a similar capacity to her predecessor, up to four motor vehicles and twelve passengers, she was fitted with two Gleniffer engines giving a speed of 7.5 knots. The new ferry was named **Dhuirnish**, after Ben Dhuirnish that rises above Bonawe. **Deirdre** was sold for further trading. Throughout her career she had operated without any major accidents, save for one incident when a lorry went overboard after its brakes failed. Fortunately the lorry sank when the ferry was at the pier and not in deep water. A result of this was that the ferry hit the pier and had to be beached by her crew, who placed a temporary patch over the hole.

1967 saw the closure of the Bonawe ferry. The workforce at the quarry had gradually been reduced with the advent of mechanisation. Following the closure of the Ballachulish branch railway line under the Beeching cuts, the Connel Bridge had become a free crossing. With a programme of road improvements the ferry service eventually became redundant and **Dhuirnish** was sold to the Bute Ferry Co Ltd in April 1967. Her turntable was removed and she was converted to a bow loader for service between Colintraive and Rhubodach, Kyles of Bute. A local resident, Donald Kennedy, operated a motorboat for the Loch Etive mail ferry, supplying outlying farms on the north shore and he was succeeded by his son, also called Donald, in 1985. A service is maintained to the present day during the summer season by a tourist ferry which leaves Taynuilt, taking passengers and supplies.

1936 TO 1939 : CONVERSION TO DIESEL

In 1935 Gardners placed an order with Scotts for their first motorship. The January 1935 AGM reported an accumulated profit of £70,123 and the Directors must have felt they were now in a position to acquire new tonnage. Launched on 22 February 1936 as *Saint Angus* (1) she sailed from Bowling on 14 April. The engine chosen was a four cylinder, 500bhp Atlas Polar engine, designed in Sweden and built under licence by British Auxiliaries Ltd, Glasgow. The company must have been satisfied with the diesel engine because they ordered a slightly larger ship completed by Scotts in March 1937 as *Saint Bedan* (1). She was also fitted with a four-cylinder Atlas Diesel built by British Auxiliaries.

Saint Angus making a smoky departure along the River Clyde.

(Bernard McCall collection)

The 1920s saw the closure of many British yards that had built steam coasters and the diesel engine was now more reliable. It offered savings in manpower and its fuel/engine weight ratio allowed an increase in cargo on a small draft. Dutch shipyards were offering very keen prices for new ships and two orders for motorships were placed in Holland. In November 1937, *Saint Ronaig* (1) was completed at Neder Hardinxveld and in March 1938 *Saint Kentigern* (1) joined the fleet having been built at Capelle a/d IJssel. The Polar engine was again chosen, but both engine units were built in Sweden by Atlas Diesel A/B. With a deadweight of 340 tonnes, *Saint Kentigern* was well suited for the smaller ports and wharves in the Irish Sea.

In 1937 *Saint Angus* loaded a number of stone cargoes at Newburgh, Fife, for Purfleet. While entering the River Thames on 17 July with one of these cargoes, her master collapsed at the wheel, suffering from food poisoning and *Saint Angus* swung to starboard, colliding with the steamer *Hartford* (407grt/12) anchored off Greenhithe. *Hartford*'s owners, F. T. Everard & Sons Ltd, sued Gardners for damage and judgement found against *Saint Angus*.

On the eve of World War 2, *Saint Conan* (1) was lost on 30 August 1939 on a voyage from Ayr to Sligo with 600 tons of coal. She sailed from Ayr on 29 August, commanded by Captain Donald Carmichael, and was put on a course to take her close to Pladda, off the southern coast of Arran, where another course change would take her towards Ireland. At midnight Captain Carmichael handed over command to the mate Mr George Moore and instructed him to change course to West South by three quarters South as the vessel passed Pladda and to stream the log. Fifteen minutes later *Saint Conan* reached Pladda and Mr Moore went below to fetch the log, leaving one of the crew at the helm. Mr Moore did not return to the bridge and *Saint Conan* continued on the course set since leaving Ayr. The course change ordered by the master on reaching Pladda was not taken and the able seaman at the helm, John McVeigh, continued to steer the same course for a further two hours.

At 02.15 hours *Saint Conan* grounded on Arranman Barrels, a reef which runs for over a half mile from the shore, in Polliwilline Bay on the south eastern shore of Kintyre. On such a fine night and with a calm sea it was not clear why Mr McVeigh did not see the approaching shore as the lights on the east coast of Kintyre would have been visible to him. *Saint Conan* struck the reef with such force that her bow reared up so high that the following day it was possible to row a small boat under her keel. After she had grounded Mr Moore was found to be asleep in the chartroom.

Several attempts were made to refloat *Saint Conan* under her own power and with the assistance of tugs. It was thought that her cargo might be unloaded to assist her salvage but the weather worsened before this could be attempted and the ship and cargo were declared a total loss. In October the steam lighter *Kinsol* sank after striking the reef while being used in salvage work on the wreck of **Saint Conan**. In December 1939, Mr Moore had his master's certificate suspended for twelve months following an inquiry. By coincidence the Judge, Sheriff Wilton, had presided over an earlier case against Mr. Moore when his certificate was suspended for twelve months in June 1937 following the loss of **Baron Polwarth** (3661grt/29) in January 1937. The inquiry found the loss of **Saint Conan** was due to the wrongful act or default of Mr Moore and Sheriff Wilton, commenting that Mr Moore's absence from the bridge was inexcusable and a serious neglect of duty, suspended Mr Moore's master's certificate from the date of the grounding.

WORLD WAR 2

At the beginning of World War 2, Gardners owned thirteen ships made up of four modern motorships averaging 2.5 years and nine steamers whose average age was 23.4 years, **Ardachy** being the oldest at thirty five. One reason for the longevity of the steamers was an increase in freight rates during 1937 which meant demand for tonnage that would normally have gone for scrapping.

The fleet traded much as normal to the end of 1939, but eventually sailed under Government orders with freight rates set slightly higher than pre-war rates by the Government. In 1940, two ships were lost and one was out of service for three months. On 26 January, **Saint Kentigern** sank in the River Mersey sailing for Londonderry. Although she was salvaged and repaired she did not return to trading until April 1940, when she sailed again with coal for Londonderry. **Saint Kearan** (1) sank eight miles south east of Pladda Light following a collision on 17 May with the French steamer **Explorateur Grandidier** (10,268grt/24). She too was bound for Londonderry, with coal from Ayr, and there was no loss of life amongst her twelve crew. The only ship lost as a result of hostilities was **Saint Ronaig**, commanded by Captain Shaw, which sank on 11 June after striking a mine as she approached Newhaven from St. Helier with a cargo of potatoes. Four of her crew were lost.

During April 1940 **Saint Angus** was chartered by Balfour Beatty Ltd to supply building materials required for improvements to the mainland airbase and Lyness naval base in the Orkney Islands. Excluding six weeks in 1941 she was on charter to Balfour Beatty until April 1944 at a fortnightly rate of £525. Within days of **Saint Angus** going on charter, the Admiralty requisitioned **Saint Oran** (2) for service as a cable ship. She was later converted to a loop layer and had a steam winch fitted to serve a bow sheave arrangement containing two rollers of three feet diameter and eight inches width. The cable was carried in the ship's hold and two port and starboard stump masts served to lift the harbour asdic equipment.

*On 3 January 1940, the Struthers' family yacht, **Hinba** (154grt/03), was requisitioned as a boom layer and then an armed patrol yacht from September 1940 to 1943. During 1942, she was used in the Examination Service to inspect neutral ships' cargoes, ensuring that the cargo was not destined for Germany. **Hinba** was sold out of Admiralty service in 1948 and it is known that she was in the Seychelles during 1956. In March of that year, she was used to ferry Archbishop Makarios to the islands from the ship which had taken him into exile from Cyprus.*

The yacht is seen here underway in Loch Linnhe.

(Company archives)

In December 1940, **Pattersonian**, a twenty five-year-old steamer, was acquired from Tyneside owners at a cost of £3,250 but was not renamed because of the Government wartime restrictions in force. She was also chartered by Balfour Beatty Ltd to supply materials for the construction of concrete blocks which formed part of the strengthening of Eastern Sound barriers in Scapa Flow. **Pattersonian** was not a stranger to war as she had rescued eleven crew from the Spanish Republican steamer **Cantabria** (5656grt/19) which had been sunk by the Nationalist auxiliary cruiser **Nadir** eight miles north of Cromer during 1933.

Scotts completed a new motorship, **Saint Rule**, in February 1941, her engine again built by British Auxiliaries Ltd. Within weeks of her completion, Balfour Beatty chartered her until November 1941 and then the Ministry of War Transport chartered her until March 1943. Another steamer joined the fleet during 1941 when **Ulster Hero** was bought from Belfast S. S. Co Ltd, part of the Coast Lines group. Again because of Government restrictions she could not be renamed.

Three ships were managed during the war for the Ministry of War Transport. **Empire Gat** was completed on the Clyde by A. & J. Inglis and was managed until 1943. Soon after her completion she was attacked by German aircraft six miles north of Trevose Head on 4 May when she was on a voyage with coal from Barry to Cowes. Damage was limited to a slight fracture of her main engine truss. **Kai** was an Estonian steamer requisitioned after the German invasion of the Baltic states in September 1941. Russian troops invaded Latvia, Estonia and Lithuania in June 1940, only for the German army to force them out in September 1941. Britain felt justified in requisitioning these countries' ships to help stem high war losses, many of which were elderly steamers employed mainly in coastal trades. **Kai** was lost with one of her crew on 1 February 1942 after she struck submerged wreckage between Trevose Head and Newquay. At the time she had been on a voyage with coal from Swansea to Southampton. Late in 1945, a third ship was managed on behalf of the Government. **Empire Congreve** was a wartime prize captured in the Channel Islands during May 1945 and as part of war reparations she was transferred to Russia in March 1946.

In 1944, **Bonawe** (2), **Saint Bedan** (1), **Saint Angus** (1), **Saint Rule** and **Saint Aidan** (1) were requisitioned for the Normandy Landings, although none was present at the beach heads on 6 June. All eventually sailed from the Solent which was one of the main staging areas for convoys to Normandy. On 8 April, **Bonawe** was requisitioned at Greenock and loaded in London, sailing on 7 June for Omaha Beach as part of Convoy ETC22W. **Saint Bedan** and **Saint Angus** were requisitioned on 17 April, **Saint Bedan** at Newport, while **Saint Angus**'s cargo book shows Balfour Beatty paying for the vessel until the end of the month even though she was off charter. **Saint Bedan** loaded at Port Talbot and joined Convoy EBC4W which arrived off Omaha Beach on 10 June while **Saint Angus** was part of Convoy ETC 5W for Gold Beach. **Saint Rule** was taken over on 27 April and loaded at Port Talbot for Omaha Beach, where she arrived about 9 June in Convoy EBC3W. **Saint Aidan** went on hire on 9 May at Cardiff after she discharged steel plates from Workington and was returned to the company on 20 June at Newport, earning £1,151 for her six weeks work.

During 1945, the requisitioned vessels were returned to the company, starting in March with **Bonawe. Saint Angus** followed in May and **Saint Bedan** and **Saint Rule** in June. **Saint Oran** was returned to the company from the Admiralty on 19 November. On 11 September 1945, **Pattersonian** stranded on the southern shore of Islay while supplying coal to various RAF bases. She was sailing around Islay's southern coast for Tiree when she grounded on the Mull of Oa. Although in a safe position her nine man crew took to the ship's boat and a Naval tug was sent from Campbeltown, but it put back because of bad weather. On 13 September, a southerly gale made her salvage impossible and she was abandoned as a total loss. Following the lifting of restrictions governing the changing of ships' names, **Ulster Hero** was renamed **Saint Conan** (2) in October 1945.

Saint Oran *was requisitioned for use as a cable ship during World War 2.* *(Bernard McCall collection)*

1945 - 1949 : THE POST-WAR PERIOD

As at the end of World War 1, the end of World War 2 was a boom time for shipowners and shipyards alike. Because Alexander Struthers was unsure if his surviving son would enter the business, the company did not order any new ships. Alexander Struthers believed that history would repeat itself and that if and when Alastair became involved in the business it might coincide with a downturn in freight rates. Newly-built ships would then become available at a fraction of their building costs allowing the company to expand at a fraction of the cost. However freight rates remained stable to 1950 and the company purchased only two second-hand steamers in the seven years after the end of the war.

While on a voyage from Glasgow with coal for Kinlochleven, **Saint Modan** (1) sank in thick fog off the west coast of Gigha, in the Sound of Jura, on 6 November 1947. She struck a rock near the island at 02.15hrs and was holed near the bow. Her skipper decided to steam at full speed to beach the vessel near Craighouse on the western shore of Jura. However the ship began to list heavily to port and sank within minutes of being abandoned by her eight crew. The twenty six-year-old steamer **Glen Mary**, which was renamed **Saint Kearan** (2) and cost £15,000 from her Aberdeen owners, replaced **Saint Modan**.

The tail shaft of **Saint Angus** (1) broke as she sailed from Newport for Fort William and Kinlochleven with alumina on 1 February 1949. She was drydocked in Cardiff with her cargo on board until 12 March when she sailed for her original destinations. During October, **Saint Kearan** spent a month at Swansea in drydock after she had to be beached when she sprang a leak while in ballast from Belfast to Cardiff. On 28 December, **Ardachy** grounded leaving Irvine for Loch Riddon and remained aground until 8 January 1950. After she was refloated she sailed to Loch Riddon and discharged her cargo of coal then returned to Irvine for repairs by Ayrshire Dockyard Co.

1950 - 1960 : FROM STEAM TO MOTORSHIP

The company remained faithful to the steam coaster when it purchased the thirty-year old **Broughty** for £6,500 from Dundee, Perth & London Shipping Co Ltd, Dundee, in May 1951. Renamed **Saint Ronaig** (2), she had been completed at Bowling by Scotts after her builders, Larne Shipbuilding Co Ltd, had gone into liquidation. Built to trade between Dundee and the Thames, she was fitted with cargo tanks in 1925 which allowed her to carry basic material used in the manufacturing of ink to the Thames, returning with spindle oil or linseed oil used in Dundee's jute mills.

*When the company bought the **Broughty**, she added a rather old-fashioned profile to the fleet. As noted above, she had previously been part of the Dundee, Perth & London Co Ltd's fleet, and had tanks fitted for the carriage of linseed oil. The tanks were fitted with heating coils and she had two cargo handling pumps salvaged from German battleships scuttled at Scapa after World War 1 fitted on deck. Both the tanks and pumps were removed before she was handed over to Gardners by whom she was renamed **Saint Ronaig** and she was the last steamer bought by Gardners.* (Bernard McCall collection)

In December 1951 **Saint Kearan** went on charter to T. S. Duff at £75 per day and sailed from Ardrossan on 29 December for the Gareloch where she was to tranship cargo from the Panamanian vessel **Maria**. In bad weather she ran aground at Ardmore Point and remained there until she was refloated on 27 February 1952 and after that she was at Irvine for repairs until 23 April. The storm that drove her aground was the same that sank the ferry **Princess Victoria** (2694grt/47) off Stranraer with heavy loss of life. This gives an indication of how far the bad weather stretched up the west coast. **Bonawe** (2) was also aground for a month while approaching Ballina with coal from Garston for the Ballina Coal Co. She remained in situ until 10 March and then spent two months at Irvine being repaired by Ayrshire Dockyard Co.

1952 saw **Ardachy** sold to the British Iron & Steel Co (BISCO) for demolition. She had been laid up at Bowling from May until September 1952, spending the rest of the year loading Irish scrap for Scottish west coast ports. She arrived in Glasgow from Bonawe for the last time on 29 December and arrived at Port Glasgow on 6 January 1953 where Smith & Houston Ltd broke her up.

During 1953, **Saint Aidan** (1) loaded two cargoes in one voyage, an unusual occurrence for the company at that time. She first loaded anchors in Devonport for Glasgow and then steel sheets in Port Talbot for Irvine which were discharged first. She spent most of June undergoing repairs at Irvine and sailed from there on 25 June. Unfortunately she grounded near Inishtrahull on the same day and had to return to Irvine where she remained until 24 August.

In November 1953, **Saint Kentigern** (1) was modernised at Bowling, the work including new navigation equipment and monkey island. In his book *Half of Glasgow's Gone*, Michael Dick describes an incident which involved **Saint Kentigern** soon after her modernisation.

Saint Kentigern *following modernisation.*   *(Bernard McCall collection)*

Just after this work was completed, she was inward bound and picked up her pilot at Gourock. He had piloted her before the alteration but this was the first experience on the renovated coaster. It was commonplace, apparently, with Gardners' ships bound for Custom House Quay, that on reaching the Broomielaw the wheel would be handed over to the pilot and the bridge personnel went below for a quick mug of tea before the ship berthed.

This occasion was no exception and the pilot was left alone on the bridge. As the city bridges loomed the pilot naturally wanted to reduce speed but to his dismay, despite frantic searching, could find no telegraph to transmit his order to the engineroom. Fortunately, before disaster struck, one of the crew reappeared on the bridge and pointed out the telegraph unit screwed to the floor, at ankle level. Economies had prevented the owners fitting the usual instrument which of course rests on a fairly long pedestal. The crewman was also able to inform the pilot that the telegraph, with a bit of practice, could be easily operated by foot control. Incidentally, other pilots using the new bridge for the first time experienced a similar lack of communication. To avoid striking the city bridges or running aground it was normal practice to arrive or sail from Custom House Quay some two hours before or after high tide. When the bridge-wing sidelight was level with a mark on the quayside wall, it was safe to sail. The usual procedure then, on many Gardners' ships which were berthed facing up river was to release the stern rope and the crew go below for refreshments. An incoming tide, surging between hull and quay, swung the stern slowly out into the river in an anticlockwise motion. By the time the tea break was over, the crew surfaced to find the ship had turned through 180 degrees and was pointing down river ready to sail ahead.

In 1954, four steamers were sold to BISCO for demolition. **Bonawe** was scrapped during April by The West of Scotland Shipbreaking Co Ltd at Troon while **Saint Oran** (2), **Saint Barchan** (2) and **Ardchattan** were allocated to Smith & Houston Ltd at Port Glasgow. The first two were delivered in the summer but **Ardchattan** received a temporary reprieve when she was bought by the Duke of Argyll & Marquis of Kintyre & Lorne for use as a depot ship in the search for a Spanish treasure ship off Tobermory.

Under the command of Rear Admiral Patrick McLaughlin RN (Rtd), the expedition consisted of five divers and six crew using **Ardchattan** as a service vessel and a hopper from Ardrossan Harbour Board was used to carry spoil away from a 10,000-yard trench. Over three months the expedition found timbers, lead sheeting, heavily concreted shot, an iron gun and some pieces of pewter plate. **Ardchattan** eventually arrived at Smith & Houston's yard in October to be broken up.

If one ship broke down there was a possibility of another company ship on hand to assist. On 5 May 1948 **Saint Barchan** grounded in the Sound of Scarba and she refloated the following day with help from **Saint Kearan** which was diverted from her voyage to Garston from Loch Aline. **Saint Aidan** and **Saint Kentigern** both sailed for Kinlochleven on 10 January 1955 from Swansea and Newport with coal and alumina. **Saint Aidan** grounded in Loch Linnhe and was helped by **Saint Kentigern** before they both berthed at Kinlochleven. **Saint Aidan** sailed on 15 January for Loch Aline to load for Garston, **Saint Kentigern** sailing the following day and she then broke down in the Irish Sea. Towed into Douglas, Isle of Man, by **Ballymena** (1,356grt/55), she was also helped by **Saint Aidan** and then spent ten days repairing in the Isle of Man before sailing for Whitehaven.

Two new motorships were ordered in 1955 from James Lamont, Port Glasgow, and the "Gideon" shipyard in Groningen, Holland. Both ships were intended to trade outside the Irish Sea and were raised quarterdeck vessels with bridge amidships and engines aft. The choice of engine was an English Electric Co Ltd 765bhp 8-cylinder turbocharged four stroke engine which belonged to the K series engine. The K series was also built for power generating plant and railway locomotives and was first fitted to the experimental LMS diesel shunters of 1934 and later in British Rail classes dating from 1956 and 1958.

Saint Aidan drydocked at Lamonts during June and July 1955 and this must have been a major decision to put her through drydocking and surveys when she was thirty-five years old and the company was disposing of its steamers. Lamonts launched **Saint Blane** on 23 June 1955 and she was handed over on 16 October, the day after **Saint Kilda** was launched at Groningen.

Saint Kilda was one of two vessels which joined the Gardner fleet in the second half of 1955.

(John Clarkson)

Saint Kilda was launched at Groningen on 15 October 1955, the day before the handing over of *Saint Blane* on the Clyde. The latter ship, seen on the right, had been launched on 23 June 1955.

(Bernard McCall collection)

During November and December, **Saint Enoch** (1) and **Saint Ronaig** (2) were lost within the space of a few weeks. **Saint Enoch** grounded on Island Magee on 23 November while in ballast from Belfast to Bonawe and was refloated on 25 November with assistance from **Flying Kestrel** (244grt/43). She was beached at Larne where it was found she had a leak in No.2 hold and she was sold to BISCO after she was declared a Constructive Total Loss. She left Larne in tow on 6 December and was broken up by Smith & Houston Ltd at Port Glasgow. On 14 December, **Saint Ronaig** was on a voyage from Garston to Westport, County Mayo, with coal and salt when she grounded in dense fog and a heavy sea at Torcar Point, south of Torr Head. The next day her eleven crew were landed by the Ballycastle Life Saving Company using breeches buoy. **Saint Ronaig** was abandoned to her insurers. Under Lloyds Open Form, Mr John Lee, of Belfast, made a salvage attempt. Due to bad weather no more attempts were made after mid-January 1956 and only a few pieces of navigational equipment were salvaged.

Age was now creeping up on some of the fleet. **Saint Angus** (1) spent the first three months of 1957 drydocked at Ardrossan and Irvine while in April **Saint Kearan** (2) was broken up at Port Glasgow by Smith & Houston Ltd. At the end of 1957, Gardners owned eight ships with an average age of 18.75 years and on 29 November 1957 were trading as follows:

Saint Aidan	sailed Loch Aline with a cargo of sand for Dublin
Saint Angus	in ballast, Manchester for Bonawe to load granite for Glasgow
Saint Bedan	on time charter to ICI since 11 July at a fixed rate of £90 per day
Saint Blane	in ballast Drogheda for Garston to load coal for Sligo
Saint Conan	unknown
Saint Kilda	loading coal at Garston for Dundalk
Saint Kentigern	on time charter to ICI from 25 November at Glasgow, at a fixed rate of £75 per day
Saint Rule	in ballast from Westport for Whitehaven to load coal for Dundalk

In February 1958, **Saint Conan** (1) was broken up at Dublin and after thirty-nine years service **Saint Aidan** (1) was sold to the same breakers the following year, sailing from Glasgow for the last time on 10 July 1959. In between these disposals Gardners saw a new motorship launched and lost. During 1956 an order had been placed with a German shipyard. The new vessel was launched in April 1958 as **Saint Ronan** (1). To finance her construction, Gardners arranged an overdraft with their bankers of £140,000, repayable at £25,000 annually. It was intended that she trade outside the Irish Sea but unfortunately she was lost with three of her crew on 11 July 1959. **Saint Ronan** was on a voyage to Rotterdam from Fleetwood with steel blooms when she collided in dense fog two and a half miles from the South Goodwin Light vessel with the Greek vessel **Mount Athos** (7176grt/43). **Saint Ronan** was hit around the port side of her Number 2 hatch and the survivors were landed at Dover. Gardners eventually won the case with no blame being attributed to **Saint Ronan** because it was later found the Greek vessel's log entries had been altered which counted against her.

The launch of **Saint Ronan** *into the River Trave at Lübeck.* *(Company archives)*

1960 – 1972 : EXPANDING HORIZONS

Gardners now owned no steamships and they continued to expand the fleet with orders for two motor ships from Dutch shipyards. Groningen's Gideon shipyard launched **Saint Brandan** (3) on 25 May 1960 which was similar in size to **Saint Ronan**. She had been ordered with the intention of working in the Baltic and North European markets and was completed in July. A smaller ship, **Saint Modan** (2), was launched on 20 July at Hoogezand and entered service in October.

Saint Kilda was another marine casualty in 1961 when she sank off Caldy Island in the Bristol Channel on 25 November. Her cargo of steel coils, loaded in Port Talbot for Glasgow, shifted and her crew abandoned her and she sank after taking on a severe list. A replacement was ordered almost immediately from the Scotstoun yard of Charles Connell & Co Ltd. The Connell family were close friends and neighbours of the Struthers family and the yard, normally associated with cargo liners, had no orders and was able to build a ship straight away. **Saint Aidan** (2) was launched in such a completed state on 26 March 1962 that she was ready for sea trials on 9 April. A year after her launch a near sister ship, **Saint Colman**, was launched at Groningen on 10 April 1963. Similar in appearance, **Saint Colman** was 13' shorter in length than **Saint Aidan** which made her suitable for the Newry coal trade as she could fit into the Newry locks. She was also named after Newry's patron saint.

*A fine view of **Saint Colman** as she was about to leave the Newry Canal via Victoria Lock on 2 July 1963. She is in immaculate condition and this would, no doubt, have been her first visit to the town after whose patron saint she was named.*

(Company archives)

Saint Kentigern (1) was sold for demolition at the end of 1963 and was broken up at Dalmuir during October. The company was also looking to replace **Saint Angus** (1) and **Saint Bedan** (1) which were now employed loading sand or granite, **Saint Angus** loading fourteen cargoes from Bonawe in April 1964. An order was placed with John Lewis & Sons Ltd, Aberdeen, for one ship, her size restricted due to the small ports within the Irish Sea and Western Isles to where she would trade. The company required a small geared vessel, measuring approximately 140' in length and because of size restrictions a 12QTM 12-cylinder Vee engine with a power/weight ratio of 13.55lg per H.P, built by W. H. Dorman & Co Ltd, was fitted. This engine was the first of two high speed engines fitted to Gardner ships, which were an unsuccessful and costly choice as they proved unsuitable for marine use. Named **Saint Fergus**, she was launched on 31 March 1964 and sailed from Aberdeen on 8 May.

Saint Bedan was handed over to Greek owners in June 1964 and served several Greek owners before she was wrecked in 1980. Greeks also bought **Saint Angus** in July 1965 and she traded until 1981 when she was stranded off Limassol. A second-hand vessel, **Oak**, was bought from the Newry & Kilkeel Steamship Co Ltd in September 1964.

*The rather severe backlighting serves to emphasise the traditional bridge-amidships profile of **Saint Bridget**. Formerly named **Oak** and a product of Scott's yard at Bowling, she was handed over at Bowling with the intention of working in the company's traditional Irish Sea trades.* *(Chriss Reynolds)*

Saint Brandan (3) collided with **Caledonian Coast** (1265grt/48) in the Mersey during 1965 while inbound from Londonderry to Weston Point with a cargo of milk powder. Although damage was not serious, **Saint Brandan** remained at Weston Point for a week undergoing repairs.

Towards the end of 1965, Gardners placed an order with Scotts for a vessel to work alongside **Saint Fergus**. Designed with a length of 150' and deadweight of 540 tonnes, she was launched on 20 January 1966 as **Saint Ronan** (2). She had the distinction of being the first ship launched on the Clyde in 1966 and the first launched by the yard since its takeover by Scotts Shipbuilding & Engineering Co Ltd, Greenock in 1965. Like **Saint Fergus**, she was fitted with a 650bhp 12QTM Dorman engine and was plagued by engine problems, having another two new engines fitted in 1968 and 1973. In November she suffered her first engine breakdown as she sailed from Southampton for Shoreham. Towed back to Southampton, she was later slipped at Bowling during December for further repairs.

*The appearance of **Saint Fergus** was not at all enhanced following the replacement of her mainmast by a crane.*

(Bernard McCall collection)

At the beginning of 1967 the company owned nine vessels with an average age of 8.7 years. On 11 January 1967 their positions were:

Saint Aidan   at Runcorn discharging sand from Antwerp
Saint Blane   sailed Dublin for Ayr to load coal for Bangor
Saint Brandan   on passage to Weston Point from Antwerp with sand
Saint Bridget   at Bowling for repairs; sailed 12 January for Garston to load coal for Bangor
Saint Colman   unknown
Saint Fergus   at Bowling for repairs
Saint Modan   sailed Creetown with granite for Glasgow
Saint Ronan   on passage to Londonderry from Garston with coal
Saint Rule   sailed Garston for Dun Laoghaire with coal

In 1966 another newbuilding was ordered from Scotts. She was launched on 26 April 1967 as **Saint William** and was fitted with a French-built 8 cylinder SEMT Pielstick engine which would give the ship more space to get 1,000 tons of coal up to Newry. The engine, although good and efficient, proved expensive in spare parts. She suffered a few breakdowns, the most spectacular one being when leaving Newry on 30 January 1968. The engine was required to go astern but a problem with the controls meant she went ahead and hit the lock gates. She remained in port until 14 February while the gates were repaired.

Saint William *underway in the River Mersey.*   *(J K Byass)*

During 1968, both **Saint Fergus** and **Saint Ronan** experienced engine breakdowns and the latter vessel lay at Bonawe for a week during September while her engine was inspected. As a result she went to Belfast for repairs before she began a charter to the Ministry of Defence at Southampton where she was used to train soldiers in the use of cargo handling equipment. In an attempt to rectify her engine problems she carried a Dorman engineer during 1969 but the problems persisted.

Saint Brandan was transferred to the ownership of Cottesbrooke Shipping Co Ltd in 1968 which was a company controlled by Charles Connell & Sons Ltd. At this time various subsidies and tax incentives made it advantageous to order new ships but a company had to be an established shipowner and not one set up specifically to take advantage of the incentives. Following the transfer of **Saint Brandan**, Cottesbrooke acquired the contract for a 16,500grt bulk carrier building on the Clyde which was launched in November 1968 as **Conon Forest** (16,781grt/69) at Upper Clyde Shipbuilders Ltd (Scotstoun Division). **Saint Brandan**'s registered ownership reverted back to Gardners the following year.

In December 1968, **Saint Rule** was handed over in Glasgow to Maltese owners and traded until 1981 when she was wrecked off Cyprus. In March and April 1969 two Norwegian ships, **Castel** (199grt/68) and **Canasta** (200grt/66), were chartered to carry sand, scrap and fertiliser cargoes around the Western Isles and a third ship, **Agnes** (NLD, 386grt/49) was voyage chartered for one cargo of sand from Loch Aline. In October 1969, Bristol Steam Navigation Co Ltd's 1953-built **Milo** joined the fleet and was renamed **Saint Angus** (2).

*The distinctive bridge design of the **Saint Angus** is very evident in this photograph. As **Milo**, she had represented the General Council of British Shipping during the Queen's Review of the Fleet at Spithead in 1953.* (Chris Witts)

On 21 March 1970, **Saint Modan** (2) was on passage from Loch Aline to Runcorn with sand when a fire broke out in her galley at 1.00am when she was one mile south of McArthur's Head Lighthouse, Islay. The fire raged for nearly six hours and put the steering gear out of action. A nearby trawler gave assistance in putting out the fire, and only the engineroom, captain's cabin and bridge were undamaged. **Saint Modan** settled down by the stern and was towed by **Saint Fergus** to Glasgow where her cargo was discharged in Queens Dock before she went to Bowling for repairs until 1 May.

Saint Bridget was transferred to another Connell subsidiary, Strathpark Shipping Co Ltd, in 1970 so that another investment grant could be obtained. Upper Clyde Shipbuilders Ltd, Scotstoun, again built the vessel which was completed as **Glenpark** (16,781grt/71). **Saint Bridget** was out of service for three weeks during 1970 when she grounded sailing from Partington and was drydocked at Manchester. Later that summer she was strikebound twice, first at Runcorn for a week and later at Gunness for three days when loaded with French grain.

While crossing Liverpool Bay in the early hours of 23 July 1970, **Saint Blane** sighted distress flares which turned out to be from the yacht **Ariadne**. **Saint Blane** stood by the yacht, awaiting the assistance of a lifeboat, but by 03.00 **Ariadne** was brought alongside and her four crew taken aboard. The yacht was later secured by a line astern and at 04.40 it was realised that the yacht was settling in the water. The master of **Saint Blane**, Captain R. A. Stuart, decided to cut the line and **Ariadne** later sank. Captain Stuart was charged with negligence resulting in the loss of **Ariadne**, although the subsequent court case found in favour of **Saint Blane**. The following year **Saint Blane** was sold to London owners and handed over in Antwerp on 26 July. She was eventually broken up in Egypt during 1979.

On 30 July 1970, Gardners signed a contract with Scotts for a vessel with delivery scheduled for early 1972. A guaranteed loan of £320,000 using **Saint Fergus** and **Saint William** as surety was taken out to cover the initial building costs. **Saint Brandan** (3) spent the first week of September 1970 at Bowling for repairs after which she sailed to load machinery in Liverpool for Antwerp. While in Liverpool, Captain Ian McKinnon took command of the ship, which sailed on 7 September. At 22.00hrs on 8 September a fire broke out while the ship was forty-five miles north north west of Trevose Head and the crew abandoned ship, later being picked up by a French trawler. The fire eventually burnt out and **HMS Cavalier** towed **Saint Brandan** into Milford Haven on 11 September. The damage was extensive and the ship was declared a constructive total loss. **Saint Brandan** was sold by her insurers for £7,300 to Dutch owners and was towed to the Continent for conversion to an inland waterways sand carrier and was later converted to suck and desalinate sand.

1972 - 1981 : A MULTI-PURPOSE FLEET

The newbuilding from Bowling was launched as **Saint Bedan** (2) on 18 January 1972 by Mrs E. P. Struthers. A gearless single-hold vessel, with portable bulkheads for cargo separation, she measured 72.2 metres in length with a deadweight of 1850 tonnes. She was fitted with a 12-cylinder Paxman engine, part of English Electric Diesel Co Ltd, and was the first company ship built with world-wide trading in mind. She was also the last ship built at Bowling for Gardners.

Saint Bridget began a two-week time charter to ICI at Irvine on 27 January and loaded nitro-glycerine for Falmouth to be transhipped to **Autolycus** (5,691grt/49). While the transfer was under way on 8 February, several cases of the cargo were found to be leaking and became unstable. Both ships were moved into Falmouth Bay and it was decided that **Saint Bridget** could not be safely unloaded and would have to be taken to sea and sunk. Under the guidance of the Department of Trade and Industry, **Saint Bridget** sailed on 14 February to a point 30 miles south of The Lizard. **Lady Roslin** (698grt/58) which took Captain P. E. Cormican and his crew off **Saint Bridget** prior to her sinking accompanied her. **Saint Bridget** did not sink immediately and was sunk by gunfire from **HMS Caprice** which had kept a watching brief on the operation. Alastair Struthers was in the Philippines acquiring land on the island of Vitilevu, Fiji, from Pacific Hotels & Developments and had to be contacted to give his permission for the vessel to be sunk. It proved difficult to contact him to agree to her being blown up.

A replacement for **Saint Bridget** was acquired during April 1972 from P. & O. Short Sea Shipping Ltd. The thirteen-year-old **Yorkshire Coast** had been built for Tyne Tees S. S. Co Ltd, part of Coast Lines, and was renamed **Saint Enoch** (2). Similar in size to **Saint Bridget**, she loaded a variety of cargoes which included household coal, sand, salt and alumina.

*A splendid view of **Saint Enoch** at Dover on 28 August 1976, presumably discharging a cargo of stone.*   *(Peter Glenn)*

On 5 April, **Saint Bedan** (2) sailed from the Clyde on her maiden voyage and loaded coal in Dublin for Portishead before ballasting to Liverpool. Here she loaded the first part of a consignment of transformers and four turbines for Puerto Rico on behalf of Vogt & Maguire. Her captain was Roddy Black, one of the company's longstanding masters, but because he had only coastal experience, he handed over command in Liverpool to Captain S. O'Mahoney who took the vessel to Puerto Rico and back. **Saint Bedan** sailed from Glasgow for Puerto Rico via the Azores where she took on bunkers. After discharging in Puerto Rico she loaded 1,444 tons of pitch in Aruba for Rotterdam at a freight rate of $16 per ton, again calling at the Azores for bunkers on the return voyage. From Rotterdam she sailed to Blyth to load coal, where Captain Black resumed command of the vessel. Gardners now owned nine ships; one was brand new from her builders and the oldest nineteen years old. The average age of the fleet was 9.1 years. On 12 May 1972, they were trading as below:

Saint Aidan	on passage from Hellvik to Manchester with sand for Colgate
Saint Angus	sailed Blyth the previous day with coal for Bangor
Saint Bedan	sailed Aruba 9 May with pitch for Rotterdam via the Azores
Saint Colman	unknown
Saint Enoch	on passage from Ardrossan to Runcorn with sand
Saint Fergus	discharging granite in two parcels at Craignure and Loch Carnan
Saint Modan	on passage Kilkieran to Bonawe with seaweed
Saint Ronan	sailed Llanddulas with granite for Glasgow
Saint William	sailed Newry in ballast for Loch Aline

In May 1973, **Saint Colman** loaded submarine cables for a freight of £13,500 in Southampton for St Johns, Newfoundland. She returned with a cargo of bagged fish meal from St Johns to Belfast, arriving there via Gridstone, Grandbank and Marystown.

The early 1970s saw great changes in the Irish Sea trades. Containerisation was evolving and ferry services offered roll-on/roll-off facilities to road hauliers, in competition with conventional cargo ships. Small ports and quays closed and coastal shipowners had to assess their ships for future markets as traditional cargoes began to disappear. Fortunately for Gardners, household coal cargoes to Northern Ireland, employing at least two of the larger vessels, would still be available for some years.

With the development of roll-on/roll-off ships, Gardners considered the possibility of constructing a small roll-on/roll-off coaster while retaining a conventional role for general trading. The company then turned to the Essex shipbuilder J. W. Cook & Co (Wivenhoe) Ltd which had designed a standard hull, marketed as the Colne type. This could be lengthened to suit individual owner's needs. All bottom plates were flat to minimise damage and reduce repair costs and the vessel could load when aground. An order was placed in 1973 for a ship with a deadweight of 560 tonnes and a loaded draught of 3.50 metres. A bow ramp allowed vehicles and plant loaded for associated Gardner companies to be carried on deck. A small crane, which ran on rails either side of the hatch coaming, was carried and the choice of engine was a Mirrlees Blackstone 637bhp, ETSL6MGR engine. Launched as **Saint Kentigern** (2) on 16 May 1973, her maiden voyage was bagged sugar from Dunkirk to Cork.

Saint Fergus and **Saint Ronan** continued to experience engine breakdowns and often required assistance from other company ships for tows to port for repairs. On 27 March 1975, **Saint Ronan** struck rocks on a voyage from Flotta to Bonawe and was towed to Bowling for repairs. She remained there until mid-June. In her absence **Isle of Rona** (436grt/56) was chartered during April to load scrap, coal and sand cargoes.

Saint Angus drydocked at Liverpool in July 1975 and then loaded grain there for Leith. After discharging there she sailed for Amsterdam but on 21 July, when she was seven miles east north east off Coquet Island on the Northumberland coast, a fire broke out in her accommodation at about 20.00hrs. **Cerdic Ferry** (2,455grt/61), **Midhurst** (1,473grt/60) and the Royal Navy frigate **HMS Eastbourne** went to her assistance, as well as an RAF rescue helicopter from the nearby RAF Acklington base. In poor visibility and driving rain a fire fighting team from **HMS Eastbourne** was landed aboard **Saint Angus** and the fire was brought under control and extinguished. The ship's cook/steward was killed in the fire and the remaining crew were evacuated to **Cerdic Ferry**, from which the helicopter took them ashore. **Saint Angus** was towed by the Tyne tug **Northsider** (156grt/67) to South Shields and repaired at Tyne Dock Engineering Ltd. She returned to service in September but was advertised for sale soon afterwards. On 25 November 1975, she was handed over to Maldives owners at Glasgow from where she sailed to Antwerp the same day and within a year she was lost off the Somali coast. Gardners made a profit of £100,000 on her original purchase price and the sale helped offset the cost of four major surveys at a time of poor freight rates. In November 1976, **Saint Enoch** was sold for £139,000, almost double her 1972 purchase price, to Cypriot owners and was eventually lost during 1986 following a collision in the eastern Mediterranean.

Saint Kentigern proved a successful ship and another order was placed for a similar, larger ship for delivery at the end of 1976. The new ship again had a bow ramp designed to take a wheeled load of up to 175 tons, with a limit of

360 tons evenly distributed on her hatch covers. Her hold was strengthened for heavy bulk cargoes such as roadstone and a portable wooden bulkhead was fitted for cargo segregation. The hatch covers were flush with the bow roadway and although gearless there was provision to fit a gantry crane. Fitted with an English Electric 6RK3CM engine she achieved 11.5 knots on her sea trials. To finance her construction a loan of £640,000 was obtained through the Shipbuilding Industry Act using **Saint William**, **Saint Bedan** (2) and **Saint Fergus** as security. **Saint Brandan** (4) was the name chosen and she was then the largest ship launched by Cooks. Lavinia, Duchess of Norfolk, was her sponsor and after the traditional bottle of champagne had been broken over her bows the ship did not move. Because of her size the river level needed to be as high as possible for another launching and she remained on the slipway until Wednesday 7 September, when a further attempt was made. Unfortunately this time she toppled to one side on the slipway and was eventually launched on Sunday 26 September. Even after these setbacks she was still handed over three weeks ahead of schedule on 8 December at Greenhithe.

*Despite the misfortunes of her launch, **Saint Brandan** has given valiant service to the company, most conspicuously in the Falklands. She was photographed at the remote Roy Cove jetty.* *(Joe McGavock)*

*In 1977 **Saint William** twice broke down requiring running repairs and **Isle of Rona** and **Turquoise** (1,143grt/61) covered a silversand and coal cargo which **Saint William** had been fixed for on each occasion. She is seen here at Bangor, Co Down, in July 1967. Bangor is one of the small Irish Sea ports which has now lost commercial traffic.*
(Ian Wilson)

To service the bulk calcium chloride contract with Alginate Industries Ltd between Winnington and the seaweed processing plant at Barcaldine, a contract was signed with Cooks on 9 May 1977 for a tanker based on the Colne hull. The engine used was a Blackstone, originally intended as a replacement for **Saint Fergus** or **Saint Ronan** should either of their Dorman engines become beyond uneconomical repair. **Saint Modan** and **Saint Ronan** had been previously used for this contract, both ships having had tanks installed in their holds to load the cargoes. A short-term loan was arranged with Alginate involved mortgaging the new tanker. She was launched as **Saint Kearan** (3) and entered service in September 1978. It was decided in 1978 to sell **Saint Modan** at the earliest opportunity and she was eventually sold in April 1979. Her cargo tanks were removed prior to her sale to new owners, who economically renamed her **Modan**.

At the beginning of 1978 the fleet stood at nine vessels and the average age of the ships had increased to 11.2 years. On 6 March 1978 they were to be found trading as follows:

Saint Aidan	discharging coal at Dundalk from Garston
Saint Bedan	sailed Hellvik for Manchester with a cargo of labradorite
Saint Brandan	sailed Kingsnorth Power Station for the Tyne after discharging preheaters
Saint Colman	loading at Ardrossan for Runcorn
Saint Fergus	sailed Northwich with soda ash for Dublin
Saint Kentigern	sailed Runcorn in ballast to load heavy lift cargo for Douglas, Isle of Man
Saint Modan	loading at Winnington for Troon
Saint Ronan	in drydock at Penzance since mid-February
Saint William	sailed Loch Aline for Ardrossan with sand

Following successful results with **Saint Brandan**, Gardners returned to the Cook yard in April 1979 with an order for a larger ship of 1,400 tonnes deadweight with delivery scheduled for June 1980. **Saint Kentigern** had also proved a versatile and profitable vessel but her career was cut short when she was lost on 3 November 1979 off West Burra Isle, Shetland. She grounded at Kettla Ness with bituminous-coated roadstone for discharge at Mid Yell on behalf of Shetland Island Council. She grounded in near hurricane conditions at 05.23hrs trying to contact the Coastguard to establish her position after she had lost her navigation aids. Captain A. McIver and five crew spent four hours in a lifeboat before they were rescued. After her loss Gardners placed another order with Cooks to replace her and as a short-term measure **Saint Fergus** took over **Saint Kentigern**'s cargoes and was fitted with a hydraulic crane.

Cooks launched the larger ship, **Saint Angus** (3), on 12 June 1980. Costing nearly £1.2 million, she was built to Lloyds Register +100 A1 class. An improved version of **Saint Brandan**, her forward goal post mast was portable and her bulwarks on either side of the ramps swung out to accept wider loads. Her hatch covers were flush with her sides, which were fitted with collapsible handrails, so that wide loads could lie over the ship's side. A second pilothouse was situated above her bridge for extra visibility when carrying a high deck cargo. Captain J. Hume, who had taken **Saint Brandan** on her maiden voyage, commanded **Saint Angus** from the builders and she sailed from Wivenhoe on 6 September. Her registered owners were Midland Montague Leasing Ltd who provided a £840,000 loan towards her building.

Saint Aidan, **Saint William** and **Saint Fergus** each went through full four-year surveys during 1979 which cost £400,000 and to help the company's cash flow it decided to sell either **Saint Aidan** or **Saint Colman** once freight rates improved. Unfortunately the surveys coincided with a downturn in trade in late 1980 and an eight week seamen's dispute in 1981 which cost the company an estimated £100,000. **Saint Ronan** and **Saint Fergus** were both sold at the end of 1980; both being valued at around £80,000 each. **Saint Ronan** was handed over on 18 December at Plantation Quay, Glasgow, to Aberdeen owners and **Saint Fergus** was sold on 28 January 1981 to Singapore owners. The fleet was now supplemented by J. & A. Gardner & Co (Management) Ltd managed vessels, the first of which was completed in September 1980 for Charles Connell & Co Ltd. Named **Craigallian**, after the Connell family's Milngavie residence, her early cargoes were UK scrap for Spain returning with French grain.

Saint Kentigern's replacement was completed in February 1981 as **Saint Oran** (3) with her building costs offset by money from the loss of **Saint Kentigern** and a loan of £760,000 using **Saint Bedan** as security. As well as a single hold for bulk cargoes and bow ramps for wheeled cargoes, **Saint Oran** was fitted with side tanks for bulk liquid calcium chloride or bulk liquid calcium bromide which allowed her to deputise for **Saint Kearan**. A two-ton travelling crane or mobile excavator could be carried to assist with cargo handling and, like **Saint Kearan**, a Schilling rudder was fitted to give a high degree of manoeuvrability in restricted waterways. Classed with Lloyds Register as a roll-on/roll-off, general cargo and chemical tanker, **Saint Oran** was the last ship built for J. & A. Gardner & Co Ltd.

In 1981, J. & A. Gardner (Management) Ltd had a short-term management contract for a refrigerated reefer, **Shereen**, which had been repossessed by her finance company. The company was responsible for her management until 1982 when she was sold to Greek owners. Taken over in New Zealand, a Gardner crew brought her back to northern Europe where she traded until her sale.

As *Saint Oran* neared completion, a contract was placed with Cooks by Glasgow salt merchants Peacock Salt Ltd for a conventional vessel based on the Colne-type hull although she differed from other Colne hulls by having a multi chine bow form. This was their first venture in shipowning having used chartered tonnage in the past. J. & A. Gardner & Co (Management) Ltd were appointed as the ship's managers. Named *Peacock Venture*, the ship was handed over on 19 February 1982 and traded on the open market around the United Kingdom and near-continent.

1982 - 2002 : CONTRACTION AND SURVIVING THE STORM

Poor freight rates continued into the 1980s and *Saint Colman* was sold to Panamanian owners in November 1981. As well as her age contributing to her sale, she had recently suffered hull damage at King's Lynn when she lay aground on a river berth at low water and had settled on a hump in the riverbed. Her sale price reflected this damage although in 1985 Gardners received £32,000 in lieu of damage after winning an arbitration hearing.

In the early hours of 23 February 1982, *Saint Bedan* was entering Lough Foyle to pick up a pilot for Londonderry at the end of a voyage from Blyth with coal. The Lough's northern shore is in the Irish Republic with a pilot station at Moville while the southern and eastern shorelines are in Northern Ireland. Unknown to *Saint Bedan*'s crew the Moville pilot station had been seized by about a dozen members of the Provisional Irish Republican Army, with the intention of using the pilot cutter to board *Saint Bedan*. The ship's crew were totally unaware of what had happened on the pilot cutter and were overpowered by the armed men who set explosive devices which detonated after the ship had been abandoned. The terrorists escaped in the pilot cutter while Captain Roddy Black and his crew rowed ashore in one of the ship's boats. *Saint Bedan* sank approximately 660 metres from Carrickarory Pier in twenty four feet of water.

The starboard side accommodation and bridge were wrecked, the engineroom was smashed and the explosion had wrecked the hatch covers resulting in the majority of the cargo being thrown out of the hold. Irish Naval divers found another unexploded device that had to be detonated, causing more damage. As she was in Irish waters at the time of the incident, a claim for £2.5million was lodged by Gardners and Lanes Derry Ltd, the cargo's consignees, representing the value of the ship and cargo. The attack came nearly a year after Coe Metcalf's *Nelly M* (818grt/72) was sunk in an identical operation while lying at anchor in Lough Foyle.

Salvage of *Saint Bedan* was awarded to P. R. Eurosalve, Folkestone, which had successfully raised *Nelly M*. Because of bad weather, preparation work to raise the vessel was delayed until May and she was not brought alongside Carrickarory Pier until 20 July. An inspection found that the salvage had been hampered by two holes on the port and starboard side of the engineroom causing hundreds of tons of silt to be deposited in the engineroom. Declared beyond economical repair, *Saint Bedan* was sold for demolition and was towed to the Mersey to be broken up there during September.

Saint Bedan's loss provided Gardners with a financial cushion against the poor freight rates. Although insured for £900,000 it would cost nearly £2 million to build an equivalent vessel and to replace her the company required another 100% on the outside freight market. *Saint Bedan* was a profitable ship, her earnings contributing towards building costs of the new tonnage coming from Cooks.

Saint Aidan was sold to West Indies owners in 1982 and following a sale drydocking was handed over on 27 May. She sailed from the Clyde on 10 June to load salt in Kilroot for Great Yarmouth and then steel props in Rotterdam for Curaçao, via Las Palmas and St Vincent.

Saint Brandan was taken on charter to work in the Falkland Islands in September 1982 and sailed from Portsmouth on 4 September, bunkering at Ascension Island on the outward journey. While off Ushant in bad weather on 6 September she lost three of five containers containing hydrochloric acid. *Saint William* was also fixed for four short term charters to the Ministry of Defence, working from Marchwood army base. She continued to be troubled by engine breakdowns and as she left Southampton to load grain in France at the end of one charter she broke down and subsequently lost the cargo. During the summer she went on charter to the MoD at Oban and broke down en route to Campbeltown, while in July she broke down fifteen miles south east of Chicken Rock and was towed into Douglas, Isle of Man, by *Ben Veen* (486grt/64).

The board had to consider whether to keep or to replace *Saint William*, which was due for a sixteen-year survey during 1983. It was eventually decided to sell the vessel. After discharging at Ardrossan in January 1984, she lay there until the end of the month when she was sold to Greek owners. Drydocked at Govan she was handed over at Yorkhill Quay, Glasgow, on 1 February and sailed for Glasson Dock to load scrap for Thessaloniki.

Saint Oran suffered an engineroom fire ten miles off the Mersey Bar on 28 April 1984 after she had left the Mersey for Norway with a cargo of mobile power units. The fire was brought under control by her crew and *Saint Oran*

*After being fitted with tanks to carry liquid calcium chloride, **Saint Modan** became a regular visitor to the Weaver Navigation which connects Northwich to the Manchester Ship Canal at Weston Point. She is seen here heading for Northwich in March 1975.*
(Neil Burns)

*Differing in style, colour and purpose from other vessels in the Gardner fleet at the time, **Solea** lies at Oban on 30 July 1990.*
(Bernard McCall)

*Clearly new at the time of this photograph, **Saint Fergus** is berthed at the riverside quay in Greenock.*

(English Electric Co Ltd)

Saint William *heads into the River Mersey at Eastham on 12 August 1983.*

(Bernard McCall)

Two further photographs taken at Eastham where the Manchester Ship Canal meets the River Mersey. Firstly, we see **Saint Kearan** approaching the locks at high water in July 1990.

(John Slavin)

With the port of Garston just visible in the distance to the left of this view, **Saint Enoch** heads towards Eastham locks in August 1975.

(John Slavin)

The Manchester Ship Canal affords excellent views of shipping, especially from the overbridges at Latchford and Warburton. **Saint Aidan** *was photographed from the latter bridge in January 1975.*   (John Slavin)

Warburton Bridge is once again the location as **Saint Bedan** *makes her way along the canal on 26 March 1976.*

(John Slavin)

*We return to Eastham once again to find **Saint Ronan** heading for the Manchester Ship Canal on a sunny June day in 1980.*
(John Slavin)

*Providing much work for the fleet in later years was the carriage of heavy loads. In 1989, **Saint Angus** makes her way cautiously down the River Cart, west of Glasgow, with cargo manufactured at the Babcock factory in Renfrew.*

(Alistair MacDonald)

*Photographed from the Connel Bridge at the start of a voyage from Bonawe to Tiree, **Saint Oran** heads westwards late on the Spring evening of 7 April 1986.*

(Bernard McCall)

returned to the Mersey under her own power where it was found that the engineroom had suffered smoke and heat damage to trunking, insulation and electrical installation. This included sound deadening equipment installed in conjunction with an experiment with the University of Essex. The following day *Craigallian* took part in a NATO exercise and went on hire at Sines, Portugal, and was returned at Gibraltar on 4 May 1984. In June *Craigallian* began a time charter and loaded explosives in Ridham Dock for Contrecoeur, Canada. After discharging this cargo she crossed the St Lawrence to load timber for Earle, New York State, and from there loaded eighteen pods on behalf of Universal Land Sea Transport for Liverpool. For the three cargoes she earned the company £29,136.

Craigallian makes ready to enter the Liverpool dock system from the River Mersey in May 1982.

(Ged Frith)

Saint Brandan was on charter in the Falklands until 1984 when she arrived back in Southampton on 28 July. She required repairs totalling £40,000 to her hatch covers and buckled coamings and was replaced in the Falklands by *Saint Angus* which had sailed from Southampton on 2 May. *Saint Angus*'s charter was with the shipbrokers Anderson Hughes who were responsible for all running costs.

Domestic coal shipments virtually ceased from May 1984 when the National Union of Mineworkers called a strike in May 1984 although a small amount of imported coal was handled at private wharves and ports outside the National Dock Labour Scheme. Gardners were fortunate to have *Saint Angus* on long-term charter, as her fuel consumption was higher than that of *Saint Brandan*. Her annual leasing charges were £175,000 and the company considered *Saint Brandan* could trade more viably around the UK than *Saint Angus*.

Because of the recession and poor freight rates it was not possible to purchase new or second-hand ships and in 1984 Gardner Shipping (Scotland) Ltd bareboat-chartered three ships from James Fisher PLC, Barrow. While this was a reversal of the fleet contraction, it was necessary at some point to add or replace tonnage in order to continue trading and the high cost of newbuildings would have virtually wiped out any potential earnings. Two sisterships built for Shamrock Shipping Co Ltd, Larne, which Fishers had recently bought, and one of Fisher's own vessels were chartered.

The Shamrock vessels, *Edgar Dorman* and *David Dorman*, were taken over on 7 March and 1 August respectively and were not renamed. The third vessel was taken over on 4 June and renamed *Loch Awe*. Completed as *Jersey Fisher*, she had been chartered to Sealink Ltd working to the Channel Islands from Southampton and Portsmouth before being chartered to Commodore Shipping Ltd and renamed *Commodore Challenger*. Almost immediately Fishers time-chartered her for a month to tranship cargo from bulk carriers anchored of Whitehaven to Albright & Wilson's Marchon chemical works, which was normally carried out by her sistership *Scafell* (829grt/71).

Edgar Dorman suffered bow and stern damage in May as she left Ayr and in June *Loch Awe* collided with another vessel when leaving Rotterdam and had to be drydocked for repairs. Both incidents cost Gardners approximately £70,000 through repairs and lost time. One of Gardner's major consignees in the Northern Ireland coal trade was Belfast-based Cawoods Fuels Ltd who approached Gardners to arrange cargoes for their two ships, *Pinewood* (1598grt/78) and *Craigmore* (1359grt/66), during the mineworkers' strike. From May 1984, Gardners acted as agents for the ships which loaded bulk cargoes in European ports for the UK and the Irish Republic including coal from Poland and Belgium to ports in the Irish Republic. When the strike ended in 1985, both ships returned to the Northern Ireland coal trade. Before the strike, the three chartered vessels had been expected to load Irish household coal and for a year this was impossible, although *Loch Awe* loaded coal in Amsterdam during August for Flixborough which was outside the National Dock Labour Scheme. Because she was on charter to Gardner Shipping (Scotland) Ltd, which was not part of the General Council of British Shipping, she was nonfederated and was thus able to load the cargo.

In June and September 1985, **Saint Oran** and **Saint Brandan** were chartered by Tolka Shipping, Dublin, to load two containers of racing pigeons in Cork for release at sea. These charters came about because of a disease amongst European racing pigeons which excluded them from British races. The Irish owners decided to hold their own races and so at a predetermined time the birds were released and the ship returned to port. Both repeated the charter twice in 1986, worth £5,200 per trip for **Saint Brandan**, while **Saint Oran** was chartered for a single run in 1987.

Saint Angus returned from the South Atlantic in 1987 and was replaced by **Saint Brandan** which sailed from Marchwood on 4 May. **Saint Angus** left the Falklands on 27 June and arrived at Southampton via Ascension Island on 16 August. In May 1988 **Saint Brandan**'s charterers became the Ministry of Defence and she remains on charter to them to the present day. The charter is for two years with an option to cancel after one year with three months notice. On 18 April 1988 **Saint Angus** was damaged after she collided with **Ever Group** (TWA, 46,551gt/86) in fog in the English Channel. The container ship continued on her way and did not stop while **Saint Angus** headed for Greenwich before going on to Sunderland for repairs to her bow and hull below her accommodation.

Peacock Venture *is seen entering the port of Blyth.*   *(Nigel J Cutts, courtesy Barry Standerline)*

At the end of 1988, **Peacock Venture** was sold to Plymouth-based owners and handed over at Milford Haven on 4 December. Built for a salt merchant, she had carried her last salt cargo in February 1984, having carried a variety of bulk cargoes and on occasions traded to Spanish and French ports. With her sale Gardners now owned a fleet of four vessels supplemented with one managed and three chartered ships. Between them their average age was ten years. On 27 June 1988, the fleet was trading as follows:

Saint Angus	sailed Hartlepool with two heavy lifts for Workington
Saint Brandan	on long-term charter to Ministry of Defence in the Falkland Islands
Saint Kearan	on passage Winnington to Ayr with bulk liquid calcium chloride
Saint Oran	loading explosives at Irvine
Craigallian	on charter to McKenzie Shipping since 10 June 1988
Loch Awe	on charter to McKenzie Shipping since 18 April 1988
Edgar Dorman	sailed Rotterdam for Londonderry with a cargo of bran pellets
David Dorman	sailed Londonderry for Coleraine to load stone for Dagenham

With the loss of all household coal cargoes in 1987, the three chartered vessels continued to trade badly and consequently affected the company's profitability. Consequently **David Dorman** was returned on 2 September and **Edgar Dorman** on 25 November. Both had been on charter to Tolka Shipping since August 1988 while **Loch Awe** and **Craigallian** had been fixed on charters to FBCA and Foster Yeoman since 1987. In April 1988, both went on charter to McKenzie Shipping Ltd, Frome. In August 1989 **Craigallian** was sold to Coe Metcalf Shipping Ltd and was handed over to them at Lowestoft while **Loch Awe** continued on charter to McKenzie Shipping until December 1990 after which she was drydocked at Greenock before being handed back to Fishers on 5 January 1991. Although the three chartered ships had been unsuccessful, one consequence was an inter-group debt of £600,000 owed by Gardner Shipping (Scotland) Ltd to J. & A. Gardner & Co Ltd. Gardners and Fishers discussed the possibility of further charters but these did not materialise.

In 1988/89, the United Kingdom Government's Tariff Reduction Scheme (TRS) subsidy for the Highlands and Western Isles was cut from 30% to 15% and this certainly did not help trade. From 1 February 1989, Gardner Shipping (Scotland) Ltd took **Saint Oran** on a twelve month charter at £700 per day in an effort to help her performance. The Board felt that by increasing the 'Scottish Presence' of the vessel they would be seen as having a commitment to the area which would lead to further work for both **Saint Oran** and the quarries.

Saint Oran and **Saint Brandan** underwent major surveys during winter of 1989/90 and because of extreme weather conditions the fleet's trading performance was affected. Consideration was given to selling **Saint Angus** and although her leasing charges fell dramatically from September 1990 it was thought the saving on bank interest charges would exceed her earning capability. A sale/leaseback arrangement from another leasing company was investigated and in February 1991 **Saint Angus** was sold to EFT Leasing Ltd and leased to Gardner Shipping (Scotland) Ltd. The sale raised £475,000 although Gardners were liable for the leasing charges. **Saint Kearan** was placed on the sales list during 1992 and although valued at £425,000 did not create any interest.

Saint Angus's running costs continued to be high, £182,300 to the year ending 31 October 1991 which included £80,000 for drydocking and surveying. On 1 June 1992, she began a two-year bareboat charter to Glenlight Shipping Ltd worth £15,500 per month and it was hoped that she would make a profit of £48,000 per year. In actual fact she made a loss of £144,300 to the year end October 1992 and at the end of the charter in June 1994 she was purchased by Glenlight's parent company, Clyde Shipping Co Ltd. Soon after her purchase Glenlight withdrew from shipowning because of the Government's reduction of the TRS and, now renamed **Glenrosa**, she was laid up. **Saint Oran** profited from Glenlight's withdrawal and now loaded round timber cargoes for Belfast and Workington, which had been **Saint Angus**'s main cargo while on charter. With the increased cargoes the possibility of purchasing a second-hand vessel was looked at, but, because of the reduced TRS, shipping in the region was not as profitable as it once had been and no ship was purchased.

After a period laid up in Greenock, **Glenrosa**, formerly **Saint Angus**, was sold and renamed **Union Saint Angus** early in 1996. After a short period trading around the coast of the UK, she left Europe in early summer and by July she was working in the Caribbean. Here she is seen in the Bristol Channel during April 1996, after departure from Avonmouth.

(Bernard McCall)

A new industry to the Western Isles in the 1980s was fish farming, mainly salmon, utilising the area's many natural lochs. Because of their remoteness they are supplied by sea and from October 1988 **Saint Oran** was involved in this trade loading fish cages and associated equipment on behalf of James Adams Ltd and Turmec International. Discharge points included places such as Loch Creran and Loch Spelve, Loch Hourn, Loch Salpin, Mallaig, Loch Cairn Bhan and Loch Claidh.

Following **Saint Oran**'s experience in the fish farm industry, a new management contract was obtained in 1990 from Golden Sea Produce Ltd, South Shian, Argyll to operate **Solea**, a live fish carrier or well-boat. **Solea** was completed in July 1989 and was initially operated by her owners before J. & A. Gardner (Management) Ltd took over her management.

Because of the growth in the fish farm industry, Gardners entered into negotiations with Lithgows Ltd who owned the shipyard at Campbeltown with a view to constructing a series of well boats to carry live fish and associated equipment. A jointly-owned company, Knapdale Shipping (Campbeltown) Ltd, was formed in August 1996 with Gardners having a 40% shareholding. Knapdale were to operate the well boats on a charter basis to third party companies with their management handled by Gardners. The first vessel, **Crear**, was completed in September 1997 and was capable of carrying approximately fifty tons of live fish in the flooded well deck. Unfortunately during 1998 the fish farm industry suffered a downturn due to a serious disease which affected the fish and their transportation and eventually **Solea**'s management contract was ended by the sale of the vessel.

At the beginning of 2001, the company operated four vessels and like other UK shipowners faced adverse trading conditions. Poor freight rates prevailed at a time when operating overheads remained constant which affected the company's viability. Work for **Crear** was spasmodic and in 1999 she was put up for sale. Although she spent some time laid up a bareboat charter was arranged for her during the year. **Saint Brandan** remained on charter to the Ministry of Defence in the Falklands and was able to pay her operating costs. Unfortunately this was not the case for **Saint Kearan** or **Saint Oran**. In general, UK coastal trading conditions were difficult although **Saint Oran** was able to find steady work towards the end of 1999. In early 2001, both **Saint Kearan** and **Saint Oran** were sold to overseas buyers. **Saint Kearan** was purchased by Norwegian owners and handed over in Norway on 25 March while **Saint Oran** sailed from Ayr on 23 April after being bought by an owner based in Newfoundland. **Crear** was returned from her charterers in 2002 and was laid up at Buckie.

It remains to be seen how long J. & A. Gardner & Co Ltd can continue as shipowners under present conditions. The company currently owns one ship which is twenty-six years old and reliant on work in the Falkland Islands. At a time when the UK's road network continues to suffer due to increased lorry traffic it is disappointing that the Government seems to do little to encourage a switch to coastal shipping and an underused rail network. Many shipping companies have ceased trading because of the changes in the industry yet Gardners survived by providing a niche service with its multipurpose vessels. With only two vessels under its control, its future would seem to be not as shipowners but as a provider of consultancy and ISM services to other owners in a world of increasing regulations.

*Fish farm equipment being discharged from the hold of **Saint Oran**.*   *(Company archives)*

BEGINNINGS . . .

In this pictorial interlude, we look at a selection of slipway, launch and trials views of some of the company's ships.

*The final preparations are being made for the launch of **Saint Brandan** (3) at the "Gideon" shipyard, Groningen, on 25 May 1960.*

(Except where stated, all photographs in this section are from company archives.)

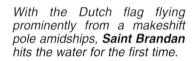

*With the Dutch flag flying prominently from a makeshift pole amidships, **Saint Brandan** hits the water for the first time.*

*Five years previously, it is the **Saint Kilda** which is being prepared for launch. The date is 15 October 1955, and coasters with bridge amidships were still very much the accepted design.*

We remain at the "Gideon" shipyard and see the **Saint Colman** a few days prior to her launch in April 1963.

(Ben Th Gernaat)

The Winschoterdiep is a waterway which runs westwards from Groningen and it is the location of several shipyards. Several of these have now closed or merged with others but shipbuilding continues to be an important industry in the area. On 20 July 1960, the **Saint Modan** (2) is ready for her official naming and launch. Onlookers are making for their favourite vantage points.

The ship has now settled in the water following her launch.

The Gardner company had traditionally been loyal to Scott & Sons yard at Bowling, and it returned there for two newbuildings in the mid-1960s. The second of these was the **Saint William** which was photographed as she slid into the water on 26 April 1967. Hatch covers remain to be fitted as part of the fitting-out process.

By contrast, the photograph below shows the **Saint Ronan** (2) shortly before her launch on 20 January 1966 and her hatch covers have already been fitted.

The **Saint Kentigern** (2) has just been launched into the River Colne at J W Cook & Sons Ltd's yard at Wivenhoe on 16 May 1973. She was the company's first purpose-built ro-ro vessel and also the first for Gardners from this Essex yard.

Having seen some vessels on or about their launch day, we now take a brief look at some trials views.

With the Dutch flag flying at her stern, the **Saint Brandan** (3) is clearly beginning sea trials off the northern coast of Holland.

Unusually for Gardners, the **Saint Fergus** was built on Scotland's east coast, her builders being J Lewis & Sons Ltd, Aberdeen.

The final coaster to be built by Scott & Sons for the Gardner company was the **Saint Bedan** (2). After a decade in service, she met a sad end after being blown up by members of the Provisional IRA. She is seen at speed off the Clyde coast, no doubt undertaking a speed trial in a measured mile.

. . . MIDDLES . . . AND ENDINGS

Although many Gardner vessels continued to trade successfully for later owners, photographs of them in subsequent ownership are surprisingly rare.

Saint William is an exception, being seen frequently in Mediterranean ports over the years. In summer 1988, she was photographed at Piraeus when named **Cleopatra Star**.

(Ralph Bigrigg)

The later names of **Saint Modan** (2) have been a source of confusion for sources suggest that she was named either **Monique** or **Monica**. In fact, both are correct and we have the evidence to prove it. Here we see **Monica** leaving Eastham on 12 August 1983. Her former fleet mate **Saint William** departed on the same tide by coincidence (see page 45).

(Bernard McCall)

Only a few weeks prior to the date of the above photograph, the same ship was observed at Exmouth under the name **Monique**. The date was 17 July 1983 and she was dischargiing tapioca pellets from Amsterdam.

(Cedric Catt)

The **Saint Ronan** of 1966 also had a subsequent name problem. She was renamed from **Helmsdale** to **Holly R** in Spring 1987 but she made only one trading voyage under this name which was never officially registered. She was scrapped at Blyth in 1990 under the name **Helmsdale** and she is seen awaiting her fate adjacent to a submarine at the scrapyard.

(Author)

Visitors to the Greek island of Zakynthos (Zante) may see a wrecked coaster in a secluded bay. Bearing the name **Panagiotis**, she began life in 1937 as Gardner's **Saint Bedan** (1). She is believed to have stranded at Zakynthos in October 1980. She features on postcards from the island, though her real history has latterly become shrouded in Greek myth! She was photographed in July 1993.

(Jim McFaul)

It was the 1972-built **Saint Bedan** which suffered the saddest end as noted on page 43. The victim of a terrorist bomb in February 1982 when only ten years old, the ship was eventually scrapped in Brocklebank Graving Dock, Liverpool. This photograph, dated September 1982, gives an indication of the damage suffered by the ship.

(John Slavin)

APPENDIX ONE : NOMENCLATURE

The first two ships ordered, **Rob Roy** and **Helen MacGregor**, were named after Robert 'Rob Roy' MacGregor (1671-1734) and his wife. After several secondhand purchases, the next new ships were named after places near to the company quarries.

Ardchattan - Priory on the north shore of Loch Etive near Bonawe.

Ardachy - A chapel near Bonawe.

Bonawe - Quarry and settlement on the southern shore of Loch Etive.

In 1910 the first ship to be named after a saint, **Saint Modan**, was completed. There is much uncertainty about many early Celtic saints. Most of the names reflect the close religious links between Ireland and Scotland in the early days of Christianity in the British Isles.

Saint Aidan - 7th century Irish saint who was the first bishop of Lindisfarne and also associated with Iona.

Saint Angus - A disciple of St. Columba, associated with Balquhidder, Perthshire.

Saint Barchan - An Irish bishop who spent his life preaching in Scotland, especially near Kilbardhan, Renfrewshire.

Saint Bedan - Alternative name for Saint Bede who founded a monastery at Jarrow.

Saint Blane - (or Blaan) 6th century bishop, born on Bute but educated in Ireland, who founded a monastery at Dunblane.

Saint Bridget - 5th century Irish abbess of Kildare.

Saint Colman - 7th century bishop of Iona and later Lindisfarne and Inisbofin (Ireland)

Saint Conan - 7th century bishop at Iona.

Saint Enoch – 10th century nun, correctly known as Saint Kennocha, revered especially in the Glasgow area.

Saint Fergus - 8th century Irish bishop who converted the pagans of northern Scotland and eventually settled in Strathearn, Perthshire.

Saint Kearan - At least 11 saints thus named. The most famous was a 6th century abbot who became one of the 12 apostles of Ireland. He established an important monastery at Clonmacnoise on the River Shannon.

Saint Kentigern - Consecrated as the first bishop of Strathclyde about 540 AD, he became the patron saint of Glasgow and is also known as Saint Mungo.

Saint Kilda - No known saint. The name probably comes from the Norse word "skildir" which means shield and may refer to the shape of a group of islands west of the Hebrides when seen from the sea and which have been named Saint Kilda.

Saint Modan - 8th century abbot associated with priory of Ardchattan.

Saint Oran - Possibly the same person as Saint Odhran, the charioteer of Saint Patrick, or Saint Otteran, a 6th century abbot of Meath who accompanied Columba to Iona.

Saint Ronaig - Unknown, possibly a variant of Saint Ronan.

Saint Ronan - One of at least 12 saints thus named, one of whom was a monk on Iona.

Saint Rule - 6th century Irish abbot

Saint William - 13th century martyr who was a native of Perth.

The names of the two ferries, **Deirdre** and **Dhurnish**. The former was the heroine of the Gaelic poem *The sons of Usnach* who eloped to Scotland from Ulster and who committed suicide after her lover was killed. **Dhurnish** named after Ben Dhurnish which rises behind Bonawe and means 'Hill of the Quarry'.

Of the managed and chartered vessels **Loch Awe** is an inland loch which drains into Loch Etive, while **Craigallian** is the Connell family residence in the Glasgow suburb of Milngavie.

APPENDIX TWO : A COMPARISON OF EARNINGS

A comparison of the voyages, cargoes and earnings of the three vessels named *Saint Angus*.

Saint Angus (1)   May 1936

	Sailed	Destination	Cargo
2nd	Glasgow	Belfast	coal
4th	Belfast	Ayr	
5th	Ayr	Larne	coal
6th	Larne	Ayr	
7th	Ayr	Larne	coal
8th	Larne	Glasgow	
10th	Glasgow	Kinlochleven	oil coke and special coke
12th	Kinlochleven	Bonawe	
13th	Bonawe	Liverpool	granite
15th	Liverpool	Paisley	rubber in cases
21st	Paisley	Glasgow	
21st	Glasgow	Londonderry	coal
22nd	Londonderry	Bonawe	
23rd	Bonawe	Glasgow	granite
25th	Glasgow	Belfast	coal
26th	Belfast	Garston	
28th	Garston	Londonderry	coal
29th	Londonderry	Bonawe	
30th	Bonawe	Glasgow	granite

Total earnings for the month : £896 14s 7d (£896.73)

Saint Angus (2)   December 1970

	Sailed	Destination	Cargo
1st	Bangor	Llanddulas	
2nd	Llanddulas	Sauda	limestone
	Sauda	Hellvik	
8th	Hellvik	Manchester	silversand
15th	Manchester	Loch Aline	
16th	Loch Aline	Runcorn	silversand
18th	Runcorn	Llanddulas	
19th	Llanddulas	Glasgow	limestone
25th	Glasgow	Dunkirk	
30th	Dunkirk	Dublin	machinery

Total earnings for the month : £10,334.26

Saint Angus (3)   May 1990

	Sailed	Destination	Cargo
1st	Craignure	Bonawe	
2nd	Bonawe	Loch Carnan	10mm crushed stone
4th	Loch Carnan	Llanddulas	
6th	Llanddulas	Thames	stone
10th	Thames	Rotterdam	
11th	Rotterdam	Le Légue	corn pellets
15th	Le Légue	Dordrecht	
18th	Dordrecht	Invergordon	palletised blasting grit
22nd	Invergordon	Montrose	
23rd	Montrose	Nigg	towers and platform
24th	Nigg	Belfast	
27th	Belfast	Shoreham	coated stone
30th	Shoreham	Le Havre	
31st	Le Havre	Swansea	one press (as ro/ro cargo)

Total earnings for the month : £60,639.17

FLEET LIST

The ship histories are arranged in chronological order according to the date they entered the Gardner fleet as newbuildings or second-hand purchases. The following abbreviations are used in the fleet list : O.N. = Official Number; g = gross registered tonnage; n = net tonnage; d = deadweight. The dimensions are overall length x breadth x summer draught. The units of measurement are those used by contemporary sources and are identified for each individual ship. Engine details are also provided. C2-cyl denotes a compound two cylinder engine, and T3 denotes a triple expansion engine. The abbreviations 2SA, 4SA etc suggest whether the engine is two stroke or four stroke and whether it is single acting or double acting. The histories of the ships have been corrected to July 2002.

Vessels owned by James Gardner, Ballachulish

1. Helen MacGregor   1876-1897   Iron
O.N. 73850   64g 44n   65.5 x 17.6 x 7.5 feet
20nhp engine by Muir & Caldwell, Glasgow

21.7.1876: Launched by Wm. Swan & Son, Maryhill, Glasgow, for James Gardner, Ballachulish. 8.1876: Completed. 1894: Transferred to the ownership of Duncan MacGregor Gardner, Glasgow. 28.11.1897: Believed to have foundered off Kerrera Island, Firth of Lorn, while on passage from Glasgow to Salen, Isle of Mull. 30.11.1897: the body of one of the crew and a lifebelt were washed up on the southern end of Kerrera Island along with other wreckage. Later that day another body, on which was found an old bill of lading for **Helen MacGregor**, was also washed up on to Kerrera Island.

2. Rob Roy   1877-1883   Iron
O.N. 76761   77g 46n   64.8 x 17.7 x 8.1 feet
16nhp steam engine by W. King & Co, Glasgow

1877: Launched by Wm Swan & Son, Maryhill, Glasgow, for James Gardner, Ballachulish as **Rob Roy**. 5.1877: Completed. 1883: Sold to Robert Moughtin, Douglas, Isle of Man. 24.11.1883: Wrecked on Carr Rock, Fife, while on passage from Greenock to Perth with general cargo. One member of her five crew was lost.

Vessels owned by Duncan MacGregor Gardner, Glasgow

3. Cuirassier   1892-1894
O.N. 28807   106g 54n   95.4 x 19.6 x 7.8 feet
25nhp engine by Carmichael & Co, Dundee

1860: Completed by Richardson, Duck & Co, Middlesbrough for John Markham, Wolverhampton, as **Cuirassier**. 1864: Sold to Wm. Rawson & Jas. Robinson, Hull. 1867: Sold to James Edward Ridlington, Boston. 1867: Sold to Boston & Hull S. S. Co Ltd, Boston. 1892: Acquired by Duncan MacGregor Gardner, Glasgow. 15.7.1894: Stranded near Cumbrae Lighthouse while on passage from Glasgow to Loch Etive with machinery. She later slipped off and sank in twelve fathoms close to the shore off Cumbrae Lighthouse. Her crew of six was saved.

Vessels owned by John Gardner & Co, later J. & A. Gardner & Co Ltd, Glasgow

4. Aston   1894-1903   Iron
O.N. 58201   132g 78n   100.0 x 20.0 x 9.5 feet
C2-cylinder by Thompson, Boyd & Co Ltd, Newcastle

20.4.1867: Launched by Schlessinger, Davis & Co, Newcastle (Yard No.10) for J. & Frederick Thompson, Queensferry, as **Aston**. 4.1867: Completed. 1879: Sold to The Aston Steamship Co Ltd, Hawarden. 1882: Sold to John Coppack, Connah's Quay. 1894: Acquired by John Gardner & Co, Glasgow. 31.01.1903: Beached at Garvel Point on the River Clyde after a collision with the steam tug **Neptune** (165grt/1893) off the entrance to the Great Harbour, Greenock whilst on a voyage from Glasgow to Bonawe with coal. Her crew of six was saved. 9.2.1903: Refloated on the evening tide and taken to Bowling for survey. Found to be beyond economical repair and broken up later that year.

5. *Norman* 1895-1897
O.N. 98621   287g 146n   136.0 x 22.1 x 10.0 feet
T3-cylinder engine by Muir & Houston, Glasgow

26.2.1891: Launched by David MacGill & Co, Irvine (Yard No. 10) for John Macfarlane, Glasgow, as ***Norman***. 4.1891: Completed. 1892: Owners became Macfarlane Shipping Co (J. Macfarlane & Co, Glasgow, managers). 1895: Acquired by John Gardner & Co, Glasgow. 1897: Sold to C. Anger, Caen, France, and renamed ***Normand***. 1903: Sold to Neau & Porsain Sainte-Marie, Ile de Ré, France. 1903: Owners became E. Neau & fils. 1905: Sold to Joseph Larran, Peyrehorade. 2.4.1914: Ran ashore in fog on Beagle Rocks near Black Head, Cornwall, while in ballast from Nantes to Fowey. The crew landed in their own boat after abandoning the vessel.

6. *Wharfinger* 1898-1911 Auxiliary
O.N. 99607   119g 68n   80.2 x 19.7 x 8.5 feet
After 1898   145g 57n   90.4 x 19.7 x 8.5 feet
C2-cylinder engine by Hedley & Boyd, North Shields

11.4.1892: Launched by Anderson & Laverick, Newcastle (Yard No. 4) for Joseph Carney, Sunderland, as ***Wharfinger***. 5.1892: Completed. 1892: Sold to J. Smurthwaite (Speeding, Marshall & Co Ltd, Sunderland, managers), Sunderland. 1893: Sold to Frederick T. Fisher, London. 1983: Sold to C.Anger, Caen, France, and renamed ***Charles***. 1898: Acquired by J. Gardner & Co, Glasgow, lengthened and renamed ***Wharfinger***. 1906: Owners became J. & A. Gardner & Co Ltd. 21.1.1911: Foundered in the Sound of Mull while on passage from Glasgow for Carbost, Skye, with a cargo of coal. Her master and five crew were lost

7. *Bonawe* (1) 1904-1917
O.N. 119082   242g 47n
116.8 x 21.6 x 9.3 feet
C2-cylinder engine by Fisher & Co, Paisley

22.10.1903: Launched by Scott & Sons, Bowling (Yard No. 166) for John Gardner & Co, Glasgow, as ***Bonawe***. 1.1904: Completed. 1906: owners became J. & A. Gardner & Co Ltd. 8.6.1917: Sank after being in collision with H. M. armed yacht ***Iolaire*** 1.5 nautical miles northeast of Point Corrie, Arran. At the time of her loss she was on a voyage from Ayr to Larne with a cargo of coal.

*****Bonawe*** approaches Bristol docks, with Brunel's Clifton suspension bridge making an unmistakable backdrop.*
(Bernard McCall collection)

8. *Ardchattan* 1907-1954
O.N. 124168   284g 65n 310d
125.5 x 22.6 x 9.7 feet
C2-cylinder engine by Fisher & Co, Paisley

18.2.1907: Launched by Scott & Sons, Bowling, (Yard No. 196) for J. & A. Gardner & Co Ltd, Glasgow, as ***Ardchattan***. 3.1907: Completed. 8.1954: Sold to Ian Douglas Campbell, Duke of Argyll & Marquis of Kintyre & Lorne, for work as a service vessel off Tobermory, Isle of Mull, while diving on the site of a wrecked Spanish galleon. 10.1954: Sold to BISCO for demolition and allocated to Smith & Houston Ltd, Port Glasgow. 21.3.1955: Register closed.

*A fine view of the **Ardchattan** underway, possibly in the Clyde estuary.   (G. E. Langmuir, Bernard McCall collection)*

9. *Ardachy*   1908-1952
O.N. 119116   210g 47n 210d   112.0 x 21.0 x 8.6 feet
C2-cylinder engine by C.Houston & Co, Glasgow

23.3.1904: Launched by Scott & Sons, Bowling, (Yard No. 170) for British Coasting S. S. Co Ltd, (Young & Gillespie, Glasgow, managers) as *Radium*. 4.1904: Completed. 30.5.1907: While in ballast from Ramelton to Glasgow struck a rock 0.5 miles west of Doherty Rock. Late that evening she was refloated and was beached 0.5 miles south-east of Lloyd's Signal Station, Malin Head. 3.6.1907: Suffered more damage during a northerly gale. 20.7.1907: Refloated but listed and settled. 25.7.1907: Refloated and taken to Malin Harbour where she was later abandoned to the underwriters as a constructive total loss. 1.1908: Acquired by J. & A. Gardner & Co Ltd, Glasgow, repaired and renamed *Ardachy*. 1952: Sold to BISCO for demolition. 6.1.1953: Arrived at Port Glasgow for breaking up by Smith & Houston Ltd, Port Glasgow.

Ardachy at Preston.   (John Clarkson)

10. *Saint Modan* (1) 1910-1947
O.N. 129468   237g 89n 280d   122.2 x 21.6 x 9.4 feet
C2-cylinder steam engine by Fishers Ltd., Paisley

13.1.1910: Launched by Scott & Sons Ltd, Bowling, (Yard No. 218) for J. & A. Gardner & Co Ltd, Glasgow as *Saint Modan*. 2.1910: Completed. 6.11.1947: Struck Gigha Island while on passage from Glasgow for Kinlochleven with coal and subsequently sank approximately 4 nautical miles south-east of Craighouse Lighthouse, Sound of Jura.

The first vessel in the fleet to be named after a Celtic saint, *Saint Modan* gave 37 excellent years service to the company. In this view, she is in the River Clyde in ballast.

(Bernard McCall collection)

11. *Saint Oran* (1) 1911-1920
O.N. 132996   237grt 89net 122.0 x 21.6 x 9.4 feet
C2-cylinder steam engine by Fishers Ltd, Paisley

9.11.1911: Launched by Scott & Sons, Bowling, (Yard No. 230) for J. & A. Gardner & Co Ltd, Glasgow, as *Saint Oran*. 12.1911: Completed. 30.12.1920: Sank between Ailsa Craig and Turnberry while on passage from Troon to Larne with coal following a collision with the steamer *Eveleen* (498grt/20).

12. *Saint Barchan* (1) 1917-1918
O.N. 137854   362g 138n   141.8 x 23.8 x 10.1 feet
C2-cylinder engine by Fishers Ltd, Paisley

3.7.1917: Launched by Scott & Sons, Bowling, (Yard No. 262) for J. & A. Gardner & Co Ltd, Glasgow, as *Saint Barchan*. 8.1917: Completed. 21.10.1918: Torpedoed and sunk 4 miles from John's Point, County Down, by *UB94* whilst on passage from Ayr to Dublin with coal. All her eight crew were lost. *Saint Barchan* was the last vessel to be sunk in British waters in World War 1 as the following day all U-boats were recalled to Germany.

13. *Saint Enoch* (1) 1918-1955
O.N. 141891   362g 138n 430d   141.8 x 23.8 x 10.1 feet
C2-cylinder steam engine by Fishers Ltd, Paisley

8.10.1918: Launched by Scott & Sons, Bowling, (Yard No. 265) for J. & A. Gardner & Co Ltd, Glasgow, as *Saint Enoch*. 11.1918: Completed. 23.11.1955: Grounded off Magee Island, County Antrim, while in ballast from Belfast to Bonawe. Five of her crew of eleven were taken off by the Donaghadee Lifeboat. 25.11.1955: Refloated by *Flying Kestrel* (244grt/43) and beached at Larne. 6.12.1955: Sailed in tow from Larne for Bowling for surveys but was later declared a constructive total loss and sold to BISCO for demolition. 12.12.1955: Arrived at Port Glasgow for breaking up by Smith & Houston Ltd.

*A fine stern view of **Saint Enoch**.*   (World Ship Photo Library)

14. *Saint Barchan* (2) 1919-1954
O.N. 141931   356g 141n 430d   141.6 x 23.8 x 10.1 feet
C2-cylinder steam engine by Fishers Ltd, Paisley

23.9.1919: Launched by Scott & Sons Ltd, Bowling, (Yard No. 283) for J. & A. Gardner & Co Ltd, Glasgow, as *Saint Barchan*. 10.1919: Completed. 6.4.1932: In collision with *Morgenen* (NOR, 7093grt/30) in the Manchester Ship Canal. 9.1954: Sold to BISCO for breaking up and allocated to Smith & Houston Ltd, Port Glasgow.

Saint Barchan

(Bernard McCall collection)

15. Bonawe (2) 1919-1954
O.N. 141937   357g 139n 430d
141.6 x 23.8 x 10.1 feet
C2-cylinder steam engine by Fishers Ltd,
Paisley

25.11.1919: Launched by Scott & Sons,
Bowling, (Yard No. 284) for J. & A.
Gardner & Co Ltd, Glasgow, as **Bonawe**.
12.1919: Completed. 1954: Sold to
BISCO for demolition and allocated to
The West of Scotland Shipbreaking Co
Ltd. 16.4.1954: Arrived at their yard at
Troon. 6.1954: Work commenced.

Bonawe *makes sedate progress in Scottish waters.*

(Bernard McCall collection)

16. Saint Aidan (1) 1920-1959
O.N. 144208   362g 138n 430d
141.5 x 23.8 x 10.1 feet
C2-cylinder steam engine by Fishers Ltd,
Paisley

4.5.1920: Launched by Scott & Sons,
Bowling, (Yard No. 286) for J. & A.
Gardner & Co Ltd, Glasgow, as **Saint
Aidan**. 7.1920: Completed. 1959: Sold to
Hammond Lane Metal Co Ltd, Dublin.
10.7.59: Sailed Glasgow to Dublin for
breaking up.

Saint Aidan *was a typical product of the Scott & Sons yard at Bowling in the
years after World War 1.*   *(J K Byass)*

17. *Saint Oran* (2) 1923-1954
O.N. 147858   253g 96n 280d   122.1 x 21.6 x 9.4 feet
C2-cylinder steam engine by Fishers Ltd, Paisley

5.5.1923: Launched by Scott & Sons Ltd, Bowling, (Yard No. 292) for J. & A. Gardner & Co Ltd, Glasgow, as ***Saint Oran***. 7.1923: Completed. 16.4.1940: Requisitioned by the Admiralty for use as a loop layer and converted for harbour defence work. 19.11.1945: Returned to the company. 1954: Sold to BISCO for demolition and allocated to Smith & Houston Ltd, Port Glasgow. 30.6.1954: Work commenced.

The company was loyal to the Scott & Sons yard as it developed its fleet in the 1920s. **Saint Oran** *dated from 1923.*
(World Ship Photo Library)

18. *Saint Brandan* (1) 1924-1928
O.N. 147936   386g 154n 430d   145 x 23.8 x 10.1 feet
C2-cylinder steam engine by Fishers Ltd., Paisley

28.10.1924: Launched by Scott & Sons, Bowling, (Yard No. 268) for J. & A. Gardner & Co Ltd, Glasgow, as ***Saint Brandan***. 11.1924: Completed. 19.10.1928: Stranded on the north-east coast of Coll during a south-westerly gale while on passage from Carbost to Glasgow with a cargo of 200 tons of barley. 20.10.1928: Abandoned by her crew of eight who were picked up by the trawler ***City of York*** (202grt/04) and landed at Tobermory. 22.10.1928: ***Bonawe*** could find no trace of the vessel which was believed to have turned over and sunk.

19. *Saint Kearan* (1) 1929-1940
O.N. 160256   691g 318n 840d   185.4 x 28.6 x 10.6 feet
T3-cylinder engine by Aitchison, Blair & Co., Ltd, Clydebank

6.6.1929: Launched by Scott & Sons, Bowling, (Yard No. 316) for J. & A. Gardner & Co Ltd, Glasgow, as ***Saint Kearan***. 7.1929: Completed. 17.5.1940: Sank 8 miles south-east of Pladda Light, Isle of Arran, on passage from Ayr to Londonderry with 800 tons of coal following a collision with ***Explorateur Grandidier*** (FRA, 10,268grt/24). Her crew of twelve was saved.

Not quite down to her marks, **Saint Kearan** appears to be loaded with coke on her forward hatch as she leaves Preston.

(World Ship Photo Library)

20. Saint Brandan (2) 1930-1935
O.N. 161924   917g 454net   199.0 x 32.1 x 12.0 feet
T3-cylinder engine by Aitchison, Blair Ltd, Clydebank

8.6.1930: Launched by Scott & Sons, Bowling, (Yard No. 318) for J. & A. Gardner & Co Ltd, Glasgow, as **Saint Brandan**. 7.1930: Completed. 21.6.1935: Grounded 5 miles south-east by east off Cape Barfleur in dense fog while on passage from Port Talbot to Rouen with coal. Refloated the same day and taken in tow by a tug for Cherbourg. 22.6.1935: Sank some 5 miles north of Cape Levi and 5 miles from Cherbourg while still under tow.

21. Saint Conan (1) 1935-1939
O.N. 140451   719g 272n 840d   188.5 x 28.7 x 11.1 feet
T3-cylinder engine by J. P. Rennoldson & Sons Ltd, South Shields

7.5.1917: Launched by J. P. Rennoldson & Sons Ltd, South Shields, (Yard No. 302) for the Hibernia S. S. Co Ltd, (J. Weatherill & Sons Ltd, Dublin, managers) as **Princetown**. 8.1917: Completed. 1935: Acquired by J. & A. Gardner & Co Ltd, Glasgow, and renamed **Saint Conan**. 1.7.1937: Grounded off Coverack while on a voyage from Rouen to Swansea in ballast sustaining damage to her stem and propeller. 30.8.1939: Grounded in Pollywilline Bay, Mull of Kintyre, while on passage from Ayr to Sligo with coal. 31.8.1939: Abandoned as a total wreck.

22. Saint Angus (1) 1936-1965
O.N. 164072   392g 193n 500d
145.0 x 23.8 x 10.5 feet
4-cylinder 2SCSA Polar oil engine by British Auxiliaries Ltd, Glasgow

20.2.1936: Launched by Scott & Sons, Bowling, (Yard No. 336) for J. & A. Gardner & Co Ltd, Glasgow, as **Saint Angus**. 4.1936: Completed. 10.7.1937: Collided with **Hartford** (407grt/12) in the Thames off Greenhithe. 1965: Sold to Adelfi Andrias, Thessaloniki, Greece, and renamed **Leon**. 1965: Renamed **Akrivoula**. 1972: Owners became Andrias Bros & Co Ltd, Thessaloniki. 1981: Sold to Mahmoud Rayes, Tripoli, Lebanon, and renamed **Hanan 1**. 23.2.1981: Vessel reported under arrest in Limassol roads, Cyprus, due to a claim for unpaid wages by the Chief Engineer. This claim was later settled and the vessel abandoned by her owners. Later a south-easterly gale drove the vessel ashore between the Old and New ports of Limassol. 8.6.1981: The vessel was still ashore and no attempt had been made to salvage her.

Saint Angus is seen at St Helier, Jersey, on 3 July 1956.

(Dave Hocquard)

23. *Saint Bedan* (1) 1937-1964
O.N. 164110   452g 245n 550d
156.8 x 25.6 x 14.0 feet
4-cylinder 2SCSA Polar oil engine by
British Auxiliaries Ltd, Glasgow

14.1.1937: Launched by Scott & Sons,
Bowling, (Yard No. 341) for J. & A.
Gardner & Co Ltd, Glasgow, as *Saint
Bedan*. 3.1937: Completed. 1964: Sold
to Gigilinis & S. Kakassinas,
Thessaloniki, Greece, and renamed
Meropi. 1965: Owners became M.
Gigilinis & D. Kalkassinas,
Thessaloniki, Greece, and renamed
Charis. 1972: Sold to Marina Koutroba
& Co, Thessaloniki, Greece. 1974:
Sold to N. S. Kalfas, Thessaloniki,
Greece, and renamed *Nicos*. 1977:
Sold to G. Trivelas & Co, (T. Katsaron,
Thessaloniki, Greece, managers) and
renamed *Panagiotis*. 1980: Sold to P.
Lisikatos & Co, Piraeus, Greece,
(Soulanis & others, Piraeus,
managers). 10.1980: Wrecked on the
island of Zakynthos (Zante) and
abandoned. The wreck was still in situ
in 1996.

*A broadside view of **Saint Bedan**. The original of this photograph was attached
to a calendar and colour tinted.*   *(Company archives)*

24. *Saint Ronaig* (1) 1937-1940
O.N. 165918   509g 268n 650d   171.5 x 27.0 x 11.5 feet
4-cylinder 2SCSA Polar oil engine by Atlas Diesel A/B, Stockholm, Sweden

10.9.1937: Launched by B V Scheepswerf & Machinefabriek "De Merwede" v/h Van Vliet & Co, Neder-Hardinxveld,
Holland, (Yard No. 378) for J. & A. Gardner & Co Ltd, Glasgow, as *Saint Ronaig*. 11.1937: Completed. 11.6.1940:
Sank after striking a mine one mile south-east of the pierhead and one mile off Newhaven west breakwater whilst
on a voyage from St Helier to Newhaven with a cargo of 520 tons of potatoes. Four of her crew were lost.

*Photographs of the 1937-
built **Saint Ronaig** are
quite rare in view of her
very short life of less than
three years. She is seen
as she was waiting to
load a cargo of Jersey
Royal potatoes at the
island's St Helier harbour.*

(Dave Hocquard)

25. *Saint Kentigern* (1) 1938-1963
O.N. 165928   249g 152n 420d   130.7 x 23.6 x 8.5 feet
4-cylinder 2SCSA Polar oil engine by Atlas Diesel A/B, Stockholm, Sweden

2.9.1937: Launched by A.Vuijk & Zonen's Scheepwerven, Capelle a/d IJssel, Holland, (Yard No. 643) for J. & A. Gardner & Co Ltd, Glasgow, as *Saint Kentigern*. 3.1938: Completed. 1963: Sold to Wm. Arnott Young & Co Ltd, Dalmuir for demolition. 18.10.1963: Work began.

Saint Kentigern was photographed arriving at Preston, probably to load coal.   (World Ship Photo Library)

26. *Pattersonian* 1940-1945
O.N. 133570   315g 119n 360d
135.3 x 23.6 x 9.1 feet
C2-cylinder engine by J. P. Rennoldson & Sons
Ltd, South Shields

16.2.1915: Launched by J. P. Rennoldson & Sons Ltd, South Shields, (Yard No. 295) for the Blaydon & London S. S. Co Ltd, Blaydon-on-Tyne, as *Blaydonian*. 3.1915: Completed. 1918: Sold to Smith, Patterson & Co Ltd, Blaydon-on-Tyne, and renamed *Pattersonian*. 1940: Acquired by J. & A. Gardner & Co Ltd., Glasgow. 11.9.1945: Stranded on the Mull of Oa, Islay, while on passage from Ayr to Port Ellen and Tiree with stores for the RAF. 13.9.1945: Boarded by salvage crews but found to be flooded throughout and abandoned as a total loss.

Pattersonian was certainly an unusual acquisition by the Gardner company. She saw service for them only during World War 2 and seems, not surprisingly, to have eluded most cameras. This rather poor photograph is, nevertheless, an important historical record.

(Bernard McCall collection)

27. *Saint Rule* 1941-1969
O.N. 166000   524g 285n 650d
166.2 x 27.1 x 9.6 feet
7-cylinder 2SCSA Polar oil engine by British
Auxiliaries Ltd, Glasgow

3.2.1940: Launched by Scott & Sons, Bowling,
(Yard No. 356) for J. & A. Gardner & Co Ltd,
Glasgow, as *Saint Rule*. 2.1941: Completed.
1969: Sold to Marine Enterprises (Malta) Ltd,
(Maltese National Lines Ltd, Valletta,
managers), Malta. 1973: Sold to Wafic
Bagdache & M. Herechie, Beirut, Lebanon, and
renamed *Mariam*. 1980: Sold to Mohamed
Karroum, Tartous, Syria, and renamed *Fourat
Star*. 3.1.1981: Arrived off Old Port Limassol,
Cyprus, from Port Said. 17.1.1981: Driven
aground on a rocky beach during a south-
westerly gale, 5 miles north of the Old Port,
Limassol. One crew member was injured. 1981:
Sold "as lies" to Epiphanious Scrap Metals who
completed demolition by 23.6.1981.

*Saint Rule is in the lock at Swansea as she prepares to leave the port
on 19 July 1964.*   *(Peter Glenn)*

28. *Ulster Hero / Saint Conan* (2)   1941-1958
O.N. 147272   483g 183n 560d   150.6 x 25.4 x 11.1 feet
T3-cylinder steam engine by J. G. Kincaid & Co Ltd, Greenock

20.5.1924: Launched by James Towers (Shipbuilding) Co Ltd, Bristol, (Yard No. 180) for Coast Lines Ltd, Liverpool,
as *Dorset Coast*. 8.1924: Completed. 1929: Transferred to Belfast S. S. Co Ltd, Belfast, and renamed *Logic*. 1935:
Renamed *Ulster Hero*. 1941: Acquired by J. & A. Gardner & Co Ltd, Glasgow. 1945: Renamed *Saint Conan*. 1958:
Sold to Hammond Lane Metal Co Ltd, Dublin, for demolition and arrived there on 9.2.1958.

*Like **Pattersonian**, **Saint Conan** was a rather
old vessel acquired during World War 2. She is
thought to have been the only ship built by the
Bristol yard of James Towers (Shipbuilding) Co
Ltd.*

(Bernard McCall collection)

29. *Saint Kearan* (2) 1947-1957
O.N. 145864   394g 148n 390d 350d   143.2 x 24.6 x 10.5 feet
T3-cylinder engine by Crabtree & Co Ltd, Great Yarmouth

11.6.1921: Launched by Crabtree & Co Ltd, Great Yarmouth, (Yard No. 183) for Wilson Bros. Bobbin Co Ltd,
Garston, (E. W. Turner, Liverpool, managers) as *Glen Mary*. 8.1921: Completed. 1929: Sold to F. T. Everard & Sons
Ltd, London. 1949: Sold to G. Couper & Co Ltd, Helmsdale. 1947: Acquired by J. & A. Gardner & Co Ltd, Glasgow,
and renamed *Saint Kearan*. 30.12.1951: Stranded at Ardmore Point. 1957: Sold to BISCO and allocated to Smith &
Houston Ltd, Port Glasgow. 6.4.1957: Arrived at their yard for demolition.

Yet another Gardner coaster at Preston, the 1921-built **Saint Kearan** arrives in ballast with three of her crew ready to secure stern lines as she prepares to come alongside. *(World Ship Photo Library)*

30. *Saint Ronaig* (2) 1951-1955
O.N. 144705   504g 200n 540d   166.1 x 25.3 x 9.6 feet
T3-cylinder engine by Wm. Beardmore & Co Ltd, Glasgow

18.5.1921: Launched by Larne Shipbuilding Co, Larne, (Yard No. 80) which ceased trading during fitting out. 10.1921: Completed by Scott & Sons, Bowling, for the Dundee, Perth and London Shipping Co Ltd, Dundee, as **Broughty**. 3.11.1921: Stranded on her maiden voyage on Abertay Sands inbound for Dundee from Hull. 23.11.1927: Sank at Kirkcaldy, Fife, after striking the pier; subsequently being refloated and taken to Leith for repairs. 1951: Acquired by J. & A. Gardner & Co Ltd, Glasgow, and renamed **Saint Ronaig**. 14.12.1955: Struck the Saddle Rock, Torcar Point, south of Torr Head, County Antrim, while on passage from Garston to Westport, County Mayo, with a cargo of salt and coal. The crew was rescued and the wreck sold to Mr John Lee, Belfast. 21.12.1955: The former steam drifter **Gossa Water** (98grt/18) stood by the wreck and a winch, Decca Navigator and R/T were salvaged. No further salvage attempts were made and the wreck was abandoned.

The oil storage tanks on the quayside provide a good clue that this yet another view at Preston. The subject on this occasion is the **Saint Ronaig** which was already thirty years old when purchased by Gardners for whom she traded for only four years before being wrecked.

(World Ship Photo Library)

31. *Saint Blane* 1955-1971
O.N. 185029   680g 318n 850d
198' 8" x 29' 4" x 12' 5½"
8-cylinder 4SCSA oil engine by
English Electric Diesels Ltd, Preston

23.6.1955: Launched by James
Lamont & Co Ltd, Port Glasgow, (Yard
No. 383) for J. & A. Gardner & Co Ltd,
Glasgow as ***Saint Blane***. 10.1955:
Completed. 23.7.1970: In the early
morning when crossing Liverpool Bay
sighted distress flares from the yacht
Ariadne while on passage from
Rouen to Silloth with a cargo of grain.
Four crew rescued. 1971: Sold to Gulf
Shipping Lines Ltd, London, and
renamed ***Gulf Planet***. 1976: Sold to
Citrine Maritime Inc, Panama and
renamed ***Zuhair***. 1978: Managers
became Gulfeast Shipmanagement
Ltd, Hong Kong. 1978: Sold to Near
East Shipbreaking Yard Company,
Egypt, and delivered at Suez for
demolition on 12.1.1979.

Saint Blane is seen at Jersey on 4 June 1970. At the time she was on charter to Huelin-Renouf for trade between the Channel Islands and Portsmouth during the potato season. *(Dave Hocquard)*

32. *Saint Kilda* 1955-1961
O.N. 185032   708g 354n 865d   197' 3" x 31' 1" x 12' 5½"
6-cylinder 4SCSA oil engine by English Electric Co, Stafford

15.10.1955: Launched by Scheepswerf "Gideon" N. V. v/h J. Koster Hzn, Groningen, Holland, (Yard No. 235) for J. & A. Gardner & Co Ltd, Glasgow as ***Saint Kilda***. 12.1955: Completed. 25.11.1961: Capsized and sank after developing a severe list four miles off Caldy Island, Bristol Channel, while on passage from Port Talbot to Glasgow with steel coils. Her nine crew took to the lifeboat and were picked up by the Angle lifeboat.

*A classic broadside view of the **Saint Kilda** as she passes Gravesend and heads for the Thames estuary.*

(Alex Duncan)

33. *Saint Ronan* (1) 1958-1959
O.N. 300202   680g 353n 875d   199' 2" x 30' 7 " x 12' 10"
8-cylinder 4SCSA oil engine by English Electric Co, Stafford

12.4.1958: Launched by Travewerft GmbH, Lübeck, West Germany, (Yard No. 224) for J. & A. Gardner & Co Ltd, Glasgow as *Saint Ronan*. 6.1958: Completed. 11.7.1959: Sank after sustaining severe damage to her port side by No. 2 hold after being in collision with *Mount Athos* (GRC, 7146grt/43) two and a half miles bearing 265 degrees from South Goodwin Lightvessel while on passage from Fleetwood to Rotterdam with a cargo of steel blooms. Three of her crew of ten were lost.

*A very rare view of the short-lived **Saint Ronan** in service. She traded for only just over a year after joining the company.*
(Bernard McCall collection)

*By contrast, the 1960-built **Saint Brandan** appears to be still sailing, albeit in a very different guise. In 1975/76, she was converted to an inland waterways vessel and current lists suggest that she now has been fitted with a Caterpillar diesel engine. They also suggest that her name should be written **Betelgeuze**. rather than **Betelgeuse** which is listed in most records. No doubt she has undergone much surgery to change her appearance from that seen in this photograph of her as **Saint Brandan**.*
(Tom Rayner)

34. *Saint Brandan* (3) 1960-1970
O.N. 301413   699g 399n 906d   196' 5" x 29' 11" x 12' 9"
5-cylinder 4SCSA oil engine by English Electric Co, Newton-le-Willows

25.5.1960: Launched by Scheepswerf "Gideon" v/h J. Koster Hzn, Groningen, Holland, (Yard No. 245) for J. & A. Gardner & Co Ltd, Glasgow, as ***Saint Brandan***. 7.1960: Completed. 1968: Transferred to the nominal ownership of Cottesbrooke Shipping Co, Edinburgh (J. & A. Gardner & Co Ltd, Glasgow, managers). 1969: Owners became J. & A. Gardner & Co Ltd, Glasgow. 8.9.1970: Suffered engineroom fire while on passage from Liverpool to Antwerp with a 140 ton electric generator. Abandoned by her crew, who were picked up by a French trawler, 44 miles north-north-west of Trevose Head, Cornwall. 11.9.1970: Fire extinguished and towed to Milford Haven by ***HMS Cavalier***. 9.1970: Sold to Metaalhandel & Sloopwerken Heuvelman-Ooltgensplaat N. A., Ouderkerk a/d IJssel, Holland for £7,300, and towed to Antwerp and then to Impe a/d Lek, where she was laid up. 1973: Sold to Hapraba N.V., Antwerp, and converted to an inland waterways sand carrier by B.V. Schps Jonker & Strans, Hendrik-Ido-Ambacht. 1975: Renamed ***Betelgeuse*** (noted as ***Betelgeuze*** in some sources). 1976: Refitted to suck and desalinate sand.

35. *Saint Modan* (2) 1960-1979
O.N. 301422   488g 244n 614d   165' 9" x 26' 7" x 11' 1$\frac{3}{4}$"
6-cylinder 4SCSA oil engine by English Electric Co, Newton-le-Willows

20.7.1960: Launched by Scheepswerf Gebr. Coops N.V., Hoogezand, Holland, (Yard No. 223) for J. & A. Gardner & Co Ltd, Glasgow, as ***Saint Modan***. 10.1960: Completed. 1979: Sold to Finekey Ltd, (Frome Shipping Co, Sutton, managers) and renamed ***Modan***. 1980: Sold to Betwood Shipping Co Ltd, (Nialed Ltd, Gravesend, managers). 1981: Renamed ***Nialed***. 1982: Sold to Naviera Jepa S. de R. L., Honduras, (Nialed Shipping Co Ltd, Gravesend, managers). 1983: Sold to Injecta Shipping S.A., Panama, (Sea River Line N.V., Derne, Belgium managers) and renamed ***Monique*** (some sources note the name as ***Monica***), with Honduras flag retained. 1984: Sold to Pegasus Inc., Panama, (Sea River Line N. V., Derne, Belgium, managers) and renamed ***Nadir***, with Honduras flag retained. 1986: Sold to Anthony Edward Combie & Edward Samson Recaii, Castries, St. Lucia, (BEP International Air Freight (St. Lucia) Ltd, Castries, St. Lucia, agents) and renamed ***Sicom***. 1996: Deleted from *Lloyd's Register*, vessel's existence in doubt.

As noted on page 14, the ***Saint Modan*** was modified to carry bulk calcium chloride. There was no hint of such modification when she was photographed as she approached the lock at Swansea on 25 August 1964, no doubt to load a cargo of coal.

(Peter Glenn)

36. *Saint Aidan* (2) 1962-1982
O.N. 301476   973g 560n 1,250d   218' 0" x 33' 7" x 13' 8$\frac{1}{2}$"
8-cylinder 4SCSA oil engine by English Electric Co, Newton-le-Willows

26.3.1962: Launched by Charles Connell & Co Ltd, Scotstoun, (Yard No. 498) for J. & A. Gardner & Co Ltd, Glasgow, as ***Saint Aidan***. 4.1962: Completed.1982: Sold to Anton Ramcharan, San Fernando, Trinidad & Tobago. 1985: Sold to Compania Cobrec S.A., Santa Domingo, Dominican Republic, and renamed ***San Andres***.   STILL IN *LLOYD'S REGISTER* (July 2002)

Saint Aidan soon gets underway as she enters the River Mersey after leaving the Manchester Ship Canal at Eastham. She is in ballast and may have delivered a cargo of silversand to the Colgate-Palmolive factory in Salford.

(J K Byass)

37. *Saint Colman*   1963-1981
O.N. 304163   917g 447n 1,230d   204' 11" x 32' 11" x 14' 6"
8-cylinder 4SCSA oil engine by English Electric Co, Newton-le-Willows

10.4.1963: Launched by Scheepswerf "Gideon" N. V. v/h J. Koster Hzn, Groningen, Holland, (Yard No. 251) for J. & A. Gardner & Co Ltd, Glasgow, as ***Saint Colman***. 6.1963: Completed. 1981: Sold to Seafaith Navigation Ltd, Panama (Barimar Shipping & Trading B.V., Spijkenisse, Holland, managers) and renamed ***Claudia P***. 1983: Sold to Penora Shipping Co Ltd, St Vincent & the Grenadines, (Ocean Fleet Trinidad Ltd, [later Ocean Freight (Trinidad) Ltd] Port of Spain, Trinidad, managers) and renamed ***Orpena***. 1991: Sold to Francois Shipping Ltd, Panama, and renamed ***Concierge***. 1993: Sold to Velda Shipping Inc, Belize City, Belize, and renamed ***Velda***. 1999: Sold to Roseda Shipping Inc, Panama City, Panama, and renamed ***St Colman*** and transferred to the Honduran register. STILL IN *LLOYD'S REGISTER* (July 2002)

*A splendid view of **Saint Colman** when newly-built. This may have been when she was on trials or it could have been the start of her delivery voyage. Unfortunately it is not possible to make out any design or lettering on the flag which is being raised on her foremast.*
(Piet Boonstra, company archives)

38. *Saint Fergus* 1964-1981
O.N. 304180   346g 171n 432d   142' 10" x 27' 1" x 10' 6"
12-cylinder Vee 4SCSA oil engine by Dorman & Co Ltd, Stafford. 3.1966: re-engined with a 12-cylinder Vee 4SCSA oil engine by Dorman & Co Ltd, Stafford

31.3.1964: Launched J. Lewis & Sons Ltd, Aberdeen, (Yard No. 345) for J. & A. Gardner & Co Ltd, Glasgow, as ***Saint Fergus***. 5.1964: Completed. 3.1966: Re-engined. 1981: Sold to Cape Elizabeth Shipping Corp, Singapore, renamed ***Cape Elizabeth*** and transferred to the Panamanian register. 1983: Sold to National Metal & Steel Corporation, Teminal Island, California, United States of America; Panamanian registry retained. 1983: Sold to United States shipbreakers. 4.8.1983: Arrived at Los Angeles for breaking up.

Saint Fergus heads into the River Mersey at Eastham on 29 September 1979, before she lost her mainmast in favour of a crane.

(John Slavin)

39. *Saint Bridget* 1964-1970
O.N. 183664   709g 358n 965d
181.6' x 31.7' x 10.8'
5-cylinder 2SCSA oil engine by British Polar Engines Ltd, Glasgow

2.12.1952: Launched by Scott & Sons, Bowling, (Yard No. 397) for the Newry & Kilkeel Steamship Co Ltd, (Joseph Fisher & Sons, Newry, managers) as ***Oak***. 4.1953: Completed. 1964: Acquired by J. & A. Gardner & Co Ltd, Glasgow, and renamed ***Saint Bridget***. 1970: Transferred to the nominal ownership of Strathpark Shipping Co Ltd, Edinburgh, (J. & A. Gardner & Co Ltd, Glasgow, managers). 8.2.1972: While transhipping a cargo of nitroglycerine at Falmouth to ***Autolycus*** (7635grt/49), it was discovered that several cases were leaking and as a safety measure both ships were moved to a safe anchorage. It was later decided that due to the unstable nature of the remaining cargo, ***Saint Bridget*** would be scuttled. 14.2.1972: Sailed from Falmouth to a point 40 miles south of The Lizard and blown up after her crew had been taken off by the escorting vessel ***Lady Roslin*** (708grt/58).

Saint Bridget *arrives at Swansea on 1 April 1967.*   *(Peter Glenn)*

40. *Saint Ronan* (2) 1966-1980
O.N. 307644   433g 204n 535d   146' 11" x 28' 4 " x 11' 1"
12-cylinder Vee 4SCSA oil engine by Dorman & Co Ltd, Stafford. 1968: Re-engined with a 12-cylinder Vee oil engine
by Dorman & Co Ltd. 1973: Re-engined with a 12-cylinder Vee oil engine by Dorman & Co Ltd.

20.1.1966: Launched by Scott & Sons (Bowling) Ltd, Bowling, (Yard No. 433) for J. & A. Gardner & Co Ltd, Glasgow
as *Saint Ronan*. 3.1966: Completed. 1968: Re-engined. 1973: Re-engined. 1980: Sold to John Coupar Simpson
and Ann Mackay Simpson, (The Northern Shipping & Trading Co (Helmsdale) Ltd, Aberdeen, managers), Aberdeen
1981: Renamed *Helmsdale*. 1987: Sold to Neil Smith, John Rigby, Peter Ham, Avi Rosenberg and Peter Howerd,
Basingstoke (CKC Shipping Services Ltd, managing agents). 25.4.1987: Arrived at Wick with a cargo of limestone
from Sunderland under the name *Holly R*. This was the only time she traded under this name which was not formally
registered. 10.9.1987: Arrived at Leith to lay up. 9.1987: Sold to Equaltrade Imports Ltd, London (Mardyke Shipping
& Chartering Ltd, Hull, managing agents). 2.1990: Sold to Andover Marine Services Ltd, Norwich, for demolition.
5.4.1990: Arrived in tow of *Mister Cornishman* (229grt/59) at Blyth to be broken up by Oceanics UK Ltd on behalf
of Andover Marine Services Ltd.

*Photographed in the River Clyde after
her launch at Bowling (see page 56),
there was no clue at that time about
the engine problems the Saint Ronan
would suffer during her career.*

*(A T Kelly & Co Ltd,
company archives)*

41. *Saint William* 1967-1984
O.N. 307679   781g 504n 1,080d   204' 2" x 31' 11" x 12' 9½"
4-cylinder Vee 2SCSA SEMT Pielstick oil engine by Chantiers de L'Atlantique, Saint Nazaire, France

26.4.1967: Launched by Scott & Sons (Bowling)
Ltd, Bowling, (Yard No. 435) for J. & A. Gardner &
Co Ltd, Glasgow, as *Saint William*. 7.1967:
Completed. 1984: Owners became J. & A.
Gardner & Co (Management) Ltd, Glasgow. 1984:
Sold to Georgis Compania Naviera S. de R. L.,
Honduras, and renamed *Sultana 1*. 1986: Sold to
Marigeorgia Compania Naviera de Honduras,
Tegucigalpa, Honduras, and renamed *Suzymar*.
1985: Renamed *Cleopatra Star*. 1989: Sold to El
Nasr Compania Naviera de Honduras S. de R. L.,
Honduras, (Cleopatra Shipping Agency,
Alexandria, managers). 1989: Managers became
A. Elias (Overseas) Co Ltd, Limassol. 1990: Sold
to Samar Wasfi Al Masri, Limassol, Cyprus, and
renamed *Tamara 1* with Honduran registry
retained. 1993: Sold to unspecified Lebanese
owners and renamed *Joella* with Honduran
registry retained. 1998: Owners identified as
Etablissement Paul Adem, Beirut, Lebanon, and
transferred to the Lebanese register.   STILL IN
LLOYD'S REGISTER (July 2002)

Saint William at Londonderry on 4 August 1974.

(Dave Hocquard)

42. _Saint Angus_ (2) 1969-1975
O.N. 185666 991g 525n 1,359d 215.7 x 33.5 x 11.7 feet
6-cylinder 2SCSA oil engine by British Polar Engines Ltd, Glasgow

15.12.1953: Launched by C. Hill & Sons Ltd, Bristol, (Yard No. 385) for the Bristol Steam Navigation Co Ltd, Bristol, as _Milo_. 3.1953: Completed. 1969: Acquired by J. & A. Gardner & Co Ltd, Glasgow, and renamed **_Saint Angus_**. 21.7.1975: Suffered a fire in her accommodation 7 miles east-north-east of Coquet Island, while on passage from Leith to Amsterdam in ballast. Her crew was taken off by **_Cerdic Ferry_** (2455grt/61) and helicopter. One crew member died in the fire. After the fire was extinguished she was taken in tow by **_HMS Eastbourne_** which later transferred the tow to **_Northsider_** (156grt/67). 22.7.1975: Arrived at South Shields for repair by Tyne Dock Engineering Co Ltd. 1975: Sold to Express Lines Shipping Co Ltd, Male, Maldive Islands, and renamed **_Lady Maria_**. 18.8.1976: Wrecked on the Somali coast off Dante, south of Ras Binnah, in a position 10.57N 51.8E while in ballast. She was later declared a constructive total loss.

Saint Angus _is loaded to her marks, possibly with coal loaded at Partington, as she passes beneath Warburton Bridge on her way down the Manchester Ship Canal._ _(John Slavin)_

43. _Saint Bedan_ (2) 1972-1982
O.N. 357470 1,251g 671n 1,950d 237' 6" x 38' 5" x 14' 5³/₄"
12-cylinder 4SCSA oil engine by English Electric Diesels, Colchester

18.1.1972: Launched by Scott & Sons (Bowling) 1969 Ltd, Bowling, (Yard No. 442) for J. & A. Gardner & Co Ltd, Glasgow, as **_Saint Bedan_**. 4.1972: Completed. 23.2.1982: While at anchor in Loch Foyle, five miles north-east of Londonderry loaded with coal, the vessel was blown up by members of the Provisional IRA after they forced the crew to abandon ship. The vessel sank in a position 55.10.30'N, 07.03 00'W. Underwater examination revealed extensive hull damage and the detonating of another unexploded device caused further damage. 21.7.1982: Arrived at Moville after being righted and refloated. 1982: Sold to Sheppards Waste Recovery Ltd, Liverpool, for demolition. 8.9.1982: Sailed for Liverpool where she arrived the following day and was subsequently broken up in the Brocklebank Graving Dock.

Saint Bedan makes a cautious approach to Irlam Locks on her way up the Manchester Ship Canal in June 1975.

(John Slavin)

44. Saint Enoch (2) 1972-1976
O.N. 186896   785grt 355net 967dwt
196' 4" x 33' 4" x 15' 3"
6-cylinder 2SCSA oil engine by British Polar Engines Ltd, Glasgow

18.6.1959: Launched by George Brown & Co (Marine) Ltd, Greenock, (Yard No. 272) for Tyne Tees Steam Shipping Co Ltd, Newcastle-upon-Tyne, as **Yorkshire Coast**. 10.1959: Completed. 1971: Managers became P. & O. Short Sea Shipping Ltd, London. 1972: Acquired by J. & A. Gardner & Co Ltd, Glasgow, and renamed **Saint Enoch**. 1976: Sold to Galwave Navigation Ltd, (Stewart Chartering Ltd, London, managers), Cyprus, and renamed **Galwave**. 1980: Sold to Ugarit Navigation Co Ltd, Cyprus, and renamed **Saer**. 13.3.1986: Sank in a position 34.13N, 34.16E after a collision with **Omar B** (891grt/65) off Cyprus while on a voyage from Beirut to Limassol with empty containers. Her crew was rescued by **Omar B**.

Saint Enoch passes Eastham as she heads towards the Manchester Ship Canal. *(J K Byass)*

45. Saint Kentigern (2) 1973-1979
O.N. 361588   469g 245n 559d   49.66 x 8.95 x 3.087 metres
6-cylinder 4SCSA oil engine by Mirrlees Blackstone Ltd, Stamford.

16.5.1973: Launched by J. W. Cook & Co (Wivenhoe) Ltd, Wivenhoe, (Yard No. 1435) for J. & A. Gardner & Co Ltd, Glasgow, as **Saint Kentigern**. 8.1973: Completed. 3.11.1979: Sank after grounding at Kettla Ness, West Burra Island, Shetland, while on passage from Bonawe to Mid Yell with a cargo of bituminous coated roadstone. Her crew of six was rescued from their lifeboat by the motorboat **Alert**.

Saint Kentigern passes Rixton on the outskirts of Warrington as she makes her way along the Manchester Ship Canal on a dull 13 May 1978. *(John Slavin)*

46. *Saint Brandan* (4) 1976-
O.N. 376968   931g 501n 1,250d   64.62 x 10.75 x 4.079 metres
6-cylinder 4SCSA oil engine by Ruston Paxman Diesels Ltd, Newton-le-Willows

26.9.1976: Launched by J. W. Cook & Co (Wivenhoe) Ltd, Wivenhoe, (Yard No. 1451) for J. & A. Gardner & Co Ltd, Glasgow, as *Saint Brandan*. 12.1976: Completed. 1984: Owners became J. & A. Gardner & Co (Management) Ltd, Glasgow. 1985: Owners became J. & A. Gardner & Co Ltd, Glasgow.   IN THE PRESENT FLEET (July 2002)

With storm clouds in the distance, *Saint Brandan* catches a shaft of sunlight as she makes her way along the Manchester Ship Canal on 9 July 1979.
(John Slavin)

47. *Saint Kearan* (3) 1978-2001

O.N. 379426   441g 180n 775d   50.42 x 9.07 x 3.331 metres
6-cylinder 4SCSA oil engine by Mirrlees Blackstone Ltd, Stamford (Engine made 1974 and fitted in 8.1978)

22.6.1978: Launched by J. W. Cook & Co (Wivenhoe) Ltd, Wivenhoe, (Yard No. 1457) for J. & A. Gardner & Co Ltd, Glasgow, as *Saint Kearan*. 9.1978: Completed. 1984: Owners became J. & A. Gardner & Co (Management) Ltd, Glasgow. 1985: Owners became J. & A. Gardner & Co Ltd, Glasgow. 16.3.01: Sold to Eide Marine Services A/S, Hoylandsbygd, Norway. Renamed *Eide Tank 1* (NIS flag). 2001: Sold to Straits Barge Co Ltd, Gibraltar, and converted for the carriage of oil. Renamed *Georgie* and transferred to Gibraltar flag. STILL IN SERVICE (July 2002)

*It was still very early on the flood tide as **Saint Kearan** made her approach to Eastham Locks in April 1996. She had, in fact, grounded briefly in the Eastham Channel just prior to this photograph. She would sail up the Manchester Ship Canal as far as Weston Point where she would join the Weaver Navigation to reach Winnington on the outskirts of Northwich. She was the last commercial vessel to use the Weaver Navigation on a regular basis.*
(Dominic McCall)

48. *Saint Angus* (3)   1980-1985
O.N. 389402   943g 611n 1,452d   64.72 x 11.23 x 3.852 metres
6-cylinder 4SCSA oil engine by Ruston Diesels Ltd, Newton-le-Willows

12.6.1980: Launched by J. W. Cook & Co (Wivenhoe) Ltd, Wivenhoe, (Yard No. 1463) for J. & A. Gardner & Co Ltd, Glasgow, as *Saint Angus*. 9.1980: Completed. 1981: Owners became Midland Montague Leasing Ltd, (J. & A. Gardner & Co Ltd, Glasgow, managers). 1984: Managers became J. & A. Gardner & Co (Management) Ltd, Glasgow. 1985 : Managers became J. & A. Gardner & Co Ltd, Glasgow. 1992: Owners became EFT Leasing Ltd, (Gardner Shipping (Scotland) Ltd, Glasgow, managers). 1994: Sold to Clyde Shipping Co Ltd, Glasgow (Glenlight Manx Ltd, Douglas, Isle of Man, managers) and renamed *Glenrosa*. 1995: Bareboat chartered to Barncrest Shipping Ltd, Wadebridge (Union Transport Group PLC, Bromley, managers) and renamed *Union Saint Angus*. 1997: Sold to Tideway Navigation Inc, Tortola, renamed *Tideway* and transferred to the St Vincent & the Grenadines register. 1998: Managers became Empresa de Navegacion Caribe, Havana, Cuba. 2000: Sold to Amblesea Ltd (Gremex Shipping S A de C V, Tampico, Mexico, managers, STILL IN SERVICE (July 2002)

Late in her career, **Saint Angus** became the subject of a link between the Gardner company and other traditional Scottish ship operating company, Glenlight, when the latter took her on charter. When photographed at Douglas, Isle of Man, on 27 June 1992, she bore the Glenlight name on her hull.

(Roy Cripps)

49. *Saint Oran* (3) 1981-2001
O.N. 389414   573g 330n 719d   53.29 x 9.17 x 3.363 metres
6-cylinder 4SCSA oil engine by Mirrlees Blackstone Ltd, Stamford.

9.12.1980: Launched by J. W. Cook & Co (Wivenhoe) Ltd, Wivenhoe, (Yard No. 1464) for J. & A. Gardner & Co Ltd, Glasgow, as *Saint Oran*. 2.1981: Completed. 1984: Owners became J. & A. Gardner & Co (Management) Ltd, Glasgow. 1985: Owners became J. & A. Gardner & Co Ltd, Glasgow. 22.4.01: Sold to Raymond Burton Berkshire, Placentia, Newfoundland. STILL IN SERVICE (July 2002)

Saint Oran in the River Mersey on a sunny day in February 1988.

(John Slavin)

VESSELS MANAGED ON BEHALF OF THE MINISTRY OF SHIPPING & THE MINISTRY OF WAR TRANSPORT

M1. *Kai*   1941
O.N. 163837   1,251g 736n   241.5 x 35.7 x 17.8 feet
T.3-cylinder engine by Nylands Værksted, Christiania (Oslo), Norway

4.1904: Completed by Nylands Værksted, Christiania (Oslo), Norway (Yard No. 142) for D/S Lom (Pedersen & Co, Christiania [Oslo], managers) as *Lom*. 1909: Sold to D/S Roskva (Erling Lund, Christiania [Oslo], managers) and renamed *Roskva*. 1915: Owners restyled D/S A/S Roskva (A. H. Arvesen, Christiania [Oslo], managers).1924: Sold to A/S Chr. Christensen, Oslo, and renamed *Torholm*. 1928: Sold to The Reval Shipping Co Ltd, Tallinn, Estonia. 1930: Company restyled Tallinna Laevauhisus A/S (The Tallinn Shipping Co Ltd), Tallinn, Estonia and renamed *Kai*. 1941: Requisitioned by Ministry of Shipping (J. & A. Gardner & Co Ltd, Glasgow, managers). 1.2.1941: Struck submerged wreckage between Trevose Head and Newquay while on a voyage from Swansea to Southampton with a cargo of coal. One crew member was lost.

M2. *Empire Gat*   1941-1942
O.N. 168674   900g 460n
203.0 x 33.1 x 11.7 feet
5-cylinder 2SCSA oil engine by British Auxiliaries Ltd, Glasgow

Empire Gat when named Borthwick.   (World Ship Photo Library)

3.11.1940: Launched by A. & J. Inglis Ltd, Glasgow, (Yard No. 1088P), for Ministry of War Transport, (J. & A.Gardner & Co Ltd, Glasgow, managers) as *Empire Gat*. 4.1941: Completed. 4.5.1941: Attacked by aircraft six miles north of Trevose Head while on passage from Barry to Cowes with a cargo of coal. She suffered damage to the main engine truss bearings. 8.1942: Managers became George Gibson & Co Ltd, Leith. 7.1947: Sold to George Gibson & Co Ltd, Leith, under the Ship Disposal Scheme and renamed *Borthwick*. 1959: Sold to Umbaldo Gennari fu Torquato & Co, Pesaro, Italy. 1960: Renamed *Agostino*. 1971: Sold to Silnari, Ancona, Italy. 1972: Sold to Ivy Shipping Co S A, Panama and renamed *Ivy*. 1986: Deleted from *Lloyd's Register*, vessel's existence in doubt.

M3. *Empire Congreve*   1945-1946
O.N. 180758   250n 119n   127.1 x 25.0 x 8.0 feet
300hp oil engine by Humbolt Deutz Moteren AG, Cologne, Germany.

7.11.1939: Launched by Schulte & Bruns, Emden, Germany, (Yard No. 136) for Wilhelm tom Worden, Hamburg, Germany as *Klaus Wilhelm*. 3.1940: Completed. 5.1945: Taken as a prize following the recapture of the Channel Islands. 10.1945: Transferred to the Ministry of War Transport, (J. & A. Gardner & Co Ltd, managers) and renamed *Empire Congreve*. 1946: Allocated as war reparations to U.S.S.R. and renamed *Koida*. 1960: Deleted from *Lloyd's Register*. No further information.

POST-WAR MANAGED VESSELS

M4. *Peacock Venture*   1981-1988
O.N. 389461   998g 617n 1,688d   67.12 x 11.26 x 4.107 metres
6-cylinder 4SCSA oil engine by Ruston Diesels Ltd, Newton le Willows

26.11.1981: Launched by J. W. Cook & Co (Wivenhoe) Ltd, Wivenhoe, (Yard No. 1468) for Peacock Salt Ltd, Glasgow, (J & A. Gardner & Co Ltd, Glasgow, managers) as *Peacock Venture*. 2.1982: Completed. 1984: Managers became J. & A. Gardner & Co (Management) Ltd, Glasgow. 1988: Sold to Sanders Stevens & Co Ltd, Plymouth, and renamed *Alila*. 1990: Sold to Bay of Bouley Ltd, (Sanders, Stevens & Co Ltd, Plymouth, managers) and transferred to the Bahamas register. 9.1992: Arrested at Plymouth in respect of mortgage held by Omega Trust Co Ltd. 12.1992: Released from arrest; chartering agents became South Coast UK Ltd, Fowey, and renamed *Alice* with Bahamas registry retained. 1993: Managers became W. D. Tamlyn & Co Ltd, Plymouth. 9.6.1995: Arrested at Teignmouth again in respect of the mortgage held by Omega Trust Co Ltd and moved to Plymouth the same day. 8.1995: Sold by order of the Admiralty Marshal to Capt. Simon Lyon-Smith, Crediton, as agent. 8.1995: Sold to Regulus Ltd, (Libra Shipping BV, Rotterdam, managers) and renamed *Bluebird* and transferred to the St Vincent & the Grenadines register. 2001: Managers became Techno Maritime Services B V, Ridderkerk, Holland. STILL IN SERVICE (July 2002)

Peacock Venture on trials.
(Company archives)

M5. *Shereen*   1981-1982
O.N. 9874-L   1,483g 857n 2,500d
80.65 x 16.24 x 5.06 metres
18-cylinder Vee 4SCSA oil engine by Normo
Gruppen A/S, Bergen, Norway

3.1.1979: Launched by Kaarbos M/V A/S, Harstad, Norway, (Yard No. 89) for P/R Fryeskip 1, Norway (Finn Khnutsen, Myre, managers) as *Nor Freeze 1*. 1979: Completed. 1980: Managers became Oivind Lorentzen A/S Sorbal, Oslo. 1981: Sold to Honeywell Maritime Corp, Panama, (Suheil Abuzeid Hableigh, Esher, managers) and renamed *Shereen*. 1981: Repossessed by her finance company and placed under J. & A. Gardner & Co Ltd management pending sale. 1982: Sold to Thurston Ltd, Bahamas (United Fleet Management Ltd, S. A. M., Monte Carlo, Monaco, managers) and renamed *Fresh Carrier*.

Azur Trader at Beverwijk on 6 December 1990.   (W H Moojen)

1988: Sold to Montague Shipping (Bahamas) Ltd., Bahamas, (United Fleet Management Ltd, S. A .M., Monte Carlo, Monaco, managers). 1989: Renamed *Azur Trader*. 1991: Sold to Riviera Shipping Ltd, Bahamas, (United Fleet Management Ltd, S. A. M., Monte Carlo, Monaco, managers). 1993: Sold to Vrissa Maritime Co Ltd, Cyprus, and renamed *Rade*. 1993: Sold to Seavic Reefer Line Inc, (Seavic Food Industries Co Ltd, managers), Samut Sakhon, Thailand and renamed *Seavic Reefer* and transferred to the Panamanian flag. STILL IN SERVICE (July 2002)

M6. *Craigallian*   1981-1989
O.N. 389400   1,494g 1,013n 2,435d   75.60 x 12.88 x 4.901 metres
12-cylinder 4SCSA oil engine by Ruston Diesels Ltd, Newton le Willows

15.7.1980: Launched by Richards (Shipbuilders) Ltd, Lowestoft, (Yard No. 548) for Charles Connell & Co Ltd, Glasgow, (J. & A. Gardner & Co (Management) Ltd, Glasgow, managers) as *Craigallian*. 9.1980: Completed. 1983: Owners became Scotstoun Shipping Co Ltd, Glasgow, (J. & A. Gardner & Co (Management) Ltd, Glasgow, managers). 1987: Owners became Charles Connell & Co Ltd, Glasgow (J. & A. Gardner & Co (Management) Ltd, Glasgow, managers). 1989: Sold to Coe Metcalf Shipping Ltd, Liverpool, and renamed *Briarthorn*. 1996: Owners became James Fisher & Sons (Liverpool) Ltd, Liverpool. 1999: Managers became James Fisher (Shipping Services) Ltd, Liverpool. 2000: Owners became James Fisher (Shipping Services) Ltd, Barrow-in-Furness. 14.2.02: Sold to O. K. Navigation, Thessaloniki, (Windward Management Ltd, Thessaloniki, managers). Renamed *O. K. Apostolos* and transferred to Panamanian flag. STILL IN SERVICE (July 2002)

A trials view of **Craigallian***.*   *(Company archives)*

M7. *Loch Awe*   1984-1991
O.N. 358157   1,537g 771n 1,516d   82.23 x 12.12 x 3.67 metres
8-cylinder 4SCSA oil engine by W. H. Allen Sons & Co Ltd, Bedford

11.1971: Launched by N. V. IJsselwerf, Rotterdam, Holland, (Yard No. 146) for James Fisher & Sons Ltd, Barrow-in-Furness as *Jersey Fisher*. 1972: Completed. 1977: Renamed *Commodore Challenger* for duration of bareboat charter to Commodore Shipping Co Ltd, St. Sampsons, Guernsey. 1981: Owners became James Fisher & Sons Public Limited Company, Barrow-in-Furness. 1983: Renamed *Jersey Fisher*. 1984: Converted to bulk carrier and renamed *Loch Awe* for duration of bareboat charter to Gardner Shipping (Scotland) Ltd, Glasgow (J. & A. Gardner & Co (Management) Ltd, Glasgow, managers). 1991: Sold to Transportes Maritimos de Portugal Ltda, Lisbon, Portugal, and renamed *TMP Aquarius*. 2001: Sold to Arados Shipping Co Srl, Constanta. Renamed *Amina Hanem* and transferred to Tonga flag. STILL IN SERVICE (July 2002)

Loch Awe *photographed at Dublin on 7 August 1987.*

(Terry O Conallain)

M8. *David Dorman*   1984-1988
O.N. 366438   664g 394n 934d   57.51 x 10.91 x 3.37 metres
6-cylinder 4SCSA oil engine by Mirrlees Blackstone Ltd, Stamford

1.4.1978: Launched by Jadewerft (Wilhelmshaven) GmbH, Wilhelmshaven, Germany, (Yard No. 143) for Shamrock
Shipping Co Ltd, Larne, (F. T. Everard & Sons Management Ltd, London, managers) as *David Dorman*. 6.1978:
Completed. 1981: Company and ship sold to James Fisher & Sons Public Limited Company, Barrow in Furness,
(F. T. Everard & Sons Management Ltd, managers). 1984: Managers became J. & A. Gardner & Co (Management)
Ltd, Glasgow, while on bareboat charter to Gardner Shipping (Scotland) Ltd, Glasgow. 11.1988: Bareboat chartered
to Dennison Shipping Ltd, Kirkwall. 1989: Renamed *Deer Sound*. 3.1994: Repossessed by James Fisher & Sons
Public Limited Company, Barrow-in-Furness, and laid up at Liverpool. 5.1994: Sold to Felix Shipping Ltd, (Alderney
Shipping Co Ltd, St. Peter Port, Guernsey, managers) and renamed *Isis* and transferred to the Isle of Man Register.
STILL IN SERVICE (July 2002)

The china clay dries at the port of Par provide a distinctive backdrop for this view of the **David Dorman** *as she waits to load
china clay on 21 July 1978.*   *(World Ship Photo Library)*

M9. *Edgar Dorman*   1984-1988
O.N. 366445   664g 393n 953d   57.51 x 10.09 x 3.37 metres
6-cylinder 4SCSA oil engine by Mirrlees Blackstone Ltd, Stamford

29.7.1978: Launched by Jadewerft (Wilhelmshaven) GmbH, Wilhelmshaven, Germany, (Yard No. 144) for Shamrock
Shipping Co Ltd, Larne (F. T. Everard & Sons Management Ltd, London, managers) as *Edgar Dorman*. 10.1978:
Completed. 1981: Company and ship sold to James Fisher & Sons Public Limited Company, Barrow-in-Furness,
(F. T. Everard & Sons Management Ltd, London, managers). 1984: Managers became J. & A. Gardner & Co
(Management) Ltd, Glasgow, while on bareboat charter to Gardner Shipping (Scotland) Ltd, Glasgow. 11.1988:
Bareboat chartered to Dennison Shipping Ltd, Kirkwall. 1989: Renamed *Bressay Sound*. 3.1994: Repossessed by
James Fisher & Sons Public Limited Company, Barrow-in-Furness. 5.1994: Sold to D. J. Goubert Shipping Ltd, Vale,
Guernsey, (F. T. Everard & Sons Management Ltd, London, managers) and renamed *Lancresse*. 4.1996: Sold to
Unicorn Ltd, (Alderney Shipping Co Ltd, St Peter Port, Guernsey, managers). 1997: Renamed *Burhou I*.   STILL IN
SERVICE (July 2002)

*This fine overhead view of the **Edgar Dorman** is undated. It is worth noting that her upperworks are painted white in contrast to the buff upperworks of the **David Dorman** in the previous photograph.* (Author's collection)

M10. Solea   1989-1998
O.N. 8818142   235g 74n 259d
33.51 x 7.61 x 3.85 metres
12-cylinder Vee 4SCSA oil engine by Caterpillar Inc, Peoria, Illinois, United States of America

22.5.1989: Launched by Campbeltown Shipyard, Campbeltown, (Yard No. 085) for Golden Sea Produce Ltd, Glasgow. 7.1989: Completed. 1996: Managers became J. & A. Gardner & Co Ltd, Glasgow. 1998: Sold to Hydro Seafoods GSP Ltd, Scalloway, Shetland. 1999: Sold to Roderick Cunningham (Scalpay) Ltd, (Highland Marine Ltd, Kyle of Lochalsh, managers). 4.2002: Laid up at Kyle of Lochalsh. 7.2002: Returned to service.

Solea is seen as she approaches Kyle in June 2001 after being slipped on the River Clyde. She has now been equipped with grading equipment on deck in order to grade the salmon at various sites. Previously she was used mainly to carry feed to the fish farms and return with a harvest. Since the photograph was taken, the deck crane has been removed.
(Alistair MacDonald)

M11. _Crear_ 1997-
O.N. 900610   381g 114n 440d   34.6 x 8.60 x 4.00 metres
8-cylinder Vee 4SA oil engine reduction geared to a single shaft by Caterpillar Inc, Peoria, Illinois, United States of America

1997: Launched by Campbeltown Shipyard Ltd, Campbeltown, (Yard No. 102) for Knapdale Shipping (Campbeltown) Ltd, Campbeltown, (J. & A. Gardner & Co Ltd, Glasgow, managers). 10.1997: Completed. 2000: Chartered to Roderick Cunningham (Scalpay) Ltd, Kyle of Lochalsh. 4.2002: Laid up at Buckie. IN THE PRESENT FLEET

Once again, Kyle provides the setting for this photograph of **Crear**.   (Alistair MacDonald)

BIBLIOGRAPHY

Song of the Clyde by Fred M. Walker, _Ferry Tales of Argyll & the Highlands_ by Walter Weyndling, _Argyll Shipwrecks_ by Peter Moir and Ian Crawford, _Clyde Shipwrecks_ by Peter Moir and Ian Crawford, _The Clyde Puffer_ by Dan McDonald, _Steam Coasters and Short Sea Traders_ by C. V. Waine, _Argyllshire & Buteshire_ by P. MacNair, _Taynuilt:Our History_ by Taynuilt Scottish Women's Rural Institute, _Hay & Company, Merchants In Shetland_ by Jas. R. Nicolson, _The 300 Year Story of Ballachulish Slate_ by Barbara Fairweather MBE, _A Short History of Benderloch, Barcaldine, Bonawe, Ardchattan and Glen Etive_ by Barbara Fairweather MBE, _Ships Monthly, Sea Breezes, Marine News, Shipbuilding & Shipping Record, Lloyd's List, Fairplay International Shipping Weekly._

ACKNOWLEDGEMENTS

With grateful thanks to: Mr Alastair Struthers, Miss Annabel Struthers, Mr Charles Struthers and the late Mr Malcolm Glen of J. & A. Gardner & Co Ltd; David Burrell (Cumnock, Ayrshire); Roy Fenton (Wimbledon); David Graham (Seaton Delaval); Gil Mayes (Launcherley); Ian Wilson (Bangor, Co Down); the Central Record Team of the World Ship Society; Argyll & Bute Library Services, Dunoon; University of Glasgow. Thanks also to the many photographers who have made their work available for publication in this book, and to the staff of Sebright Printers.

INDEX OF SHIP'S NAMES

In the following list, all ships owned or managed by J & A Gardner & Co Ltd and its predecessors are written in bold italics. Earlier or later names of such ships are written in italics. The names of all other vessels mentioned in the text are written in ordinary lettering.

Ship's Name	Fleet List No.	Pages	Ship's Name	Fleet List No.	Pages
Morgenen		27,65			45,57,77
Mount Athos		34,74	*Saint Kearan* (1)	19	27,29,67
Nadir		29	*Saint Kearan* (2)	29	22,31-34,71,72
Nadir	35	75	*Saint Kearan* (3)	47	9,14,15,42,46,51-53,82
Nelly M	43		*Saint Kentigern* (1)	25	13,14,21,22,28,29,32,
Neptune		24,62			33,35,70
Nialed	35	75	*Saint Kentigern* (2)	45	10,11,17-21,40,42,56,
Nicos	23	69			80,81
Nor Freeze 1	M5	85	*Saint Kilda*	32	14,23,33,35,54,73
Norman	5	24,63	*Saint Modan* (1)	10	5,13,24-26,31,64
Normand	5	63	*Saint Modan* (2)	35	9,14,15,35,37,38,40,
Northsider		40,79			42,44,55,58,75
O. K. Apostolos	M6	86	*Saint Oran* (1)	11	25,26,64
Oak	39	35,36,77	*Saint Oran* (2)	17	25,26,29,32,67
Odysseus		21	*Saint Oran* (3)	49	8,9,11,12,14,15,22,42,
Omar B		80			43,49,51-53,83
Orpena	37	76	*Saint Ronaig* (1)	24	28,29,69
Panagiotis	23	59,69	*Saint Ronaig* (2)	30	31,34,72
Pattersonian	26	29,30,70,71	*Saint Ronan* (1)	33	34,35,74
Peacock Venture	M4	43,51,85	*Saint Ronan* (2)	40	6,9,10,13,14,18,20,21,
Pinewood		50			36,37,40,42,48,56,59,
Princess Victoria		32			78
Princetown	21	27,68	*Saint Rule*	27	14,21,22,29,30,37,38,
Rade	M5	85			71
Radium	9	24	*Saint William*	41	12,13,16,37,38,40-43,
Raider (HMS)		18			45,56,58,78
Rob Roy	2	24,62	San Andres	36	75
Roskva	M1	84	Scafell		50
Saer	44	80	Seavic Reefer	M5	85
Saint Aidan (1)	16	14,21,22,25,30,32,33,	Sicom	35	75
		34,66	**Shereen**	M5	42,85
Saint Aidan (2)	36	12,13,16,18,23,35,37,	**Solea**	M10	44,53,88
		40,42,43,47,75,76	St Colman	37	76
Saint Angus (1)	22	16,21,22,28,29,30,31,	Stridence		23
		34,35,61,68	Sugar Producer		23
Saint Angus (2)	42	12,13,16,18,38,40,48,	Sultana 1	41	78
		61,79	Suzymar	41	78
Saint Angus (3)	48	7,8,14,18,19,50,51,52,	Tamara 1	41	78
		61,82,83	Tideway	48	82
Saint Barchan (1)	12	25,27,65	*TMP Aquarius*	M7	86
Saint Barchan (2)	14	25,26,32,33,65	Torholm	M1	84
Saint Bedan (1)	23	13,14,21,22,28,30,35,	Tracker (HMS)		18
		59,69	Turquoise		41
Saint Bedan (2)	43	13,14,16,18,39-43,47,	UB94		25,65
		57,59,79,80	**Ulster Hero**	28	29,30,71
Saint Blane	31	14,33,37,38,73	Union Saint Angus	48	52,82
Saint Brandan (1)	18	26,27,67	Velda	37	76
Saint Brandan (2)	20	27,68	Vic 85		11
Saint Brandan (3)	34	12,16,23,35-39,54,57,	Vivanita		22
		74,75	Wegro		12
Saint Brandan (4)	46	7,9,14,18,19,41-43,	**Wharfinger**	6	4,24,63
		50-53,81	Wib		21
Saint Bridget	39	22,36-39,77	Wiggs		21
Saint Colman	37	12,17,35,37,40,42,43,	Wilks		21
		55,76	Wis		21
Saint Conan (1)	21	27,28,29,34,68	Wopper		21
Saint Conan (2)	28	30,71	Yorkshire Coast	44	39,80
Saint Enoch (1)	13	25,34,65	Zephyr 1		21
Saint Enoch (2)	44	39,40,46,80	Zuhair	31	73
Saint Fergus	38	6,10,13,35-38,40-42,			